OLD
Silver Spoons
OF ENGLAND

PLATE I

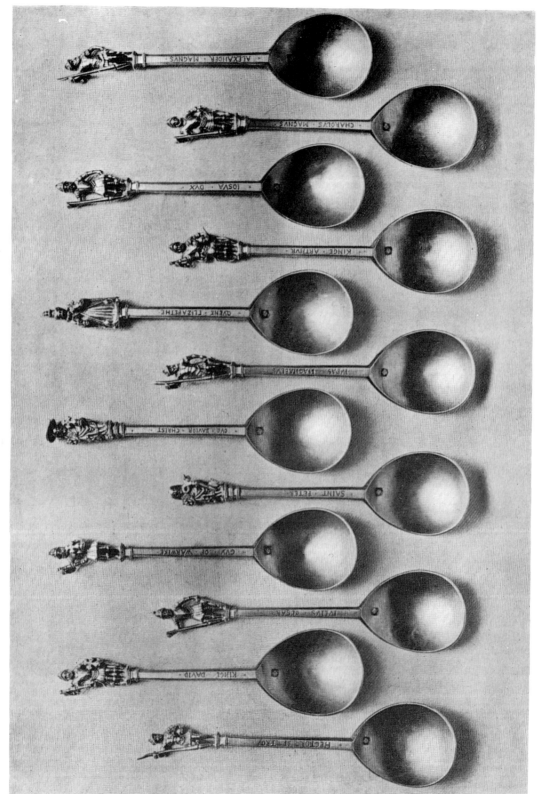

Sir Joseph Tichborne's famous Elizabethan "Celebrities" set of Silver-gilt Terminal Figure Spoons.

The only set of its kind known, which was sold at Christie's in June, 1914, for £2,000.

Date: London, 1592-3. Maker's mark, a Crescent enclosing W.

Names shown on stems. For further details see text.

OLD
Silver Spoons
OF ENGLAND

Norman Gask

Spring Books
London · New York · Sydney · Toronto

Original edition published 1926 by
Herbert Jenkins Limited, London
All rights reserved
This edition published 1973 by
The Hamlyn Publishing Group Limited
London · New York · Sydney · Toronto
Hamlyn House, Feltham, Middlesex, England

ISBN 0 600 36717 7

Printed in England by
The Chapel River Press, Andover

TO JOHN

Publishers note to the 1973 edition

This book is presented in its original form, as published in 1926, complete and unabridged.

OLD SILVER SPOONS

Old Silver Spoons! Old Silver Spoons!
What storied pasts your magic croons.
What christenings at Tudor noons,
Of babes gone now three thousand moons.
      Old Silver Spoons!

What tales of towers, what banquet tunes,
What fairy bells and fragrant runes
Of lives and loves in far-off Junes—
      Old Silver Spoons!

Proud Lion Sejant of Queen Bess,
Shy Maydenhedde that shows the dress,
Slim Akernes, Spearheads, Wrythen-Knops,
Apostles, Slipped-ends, staid Seal-tops,
Plain Puritans of Cromwell's age,
Lobed-ends and Rat-tails close the page.
      Old Silver Spoons!

INTRODUCTION

THE astonishing discovery that no book is published which devotes more than a relatively few pages to the wide subject of old English silver spoons, and the fascination of these homely relics, which reflect so much of the historic art and craftsmanship of this country before the coming of mechanical production, have led me to attempt the present volume.

The need of some practical guide, enriched with actual photographs, has been frequently suggested by the amateur and professional collectors from all over the country, who throng the salesrooms at Christie's and elsewhere whenever an auction of old English silver spoons is announced, and often bid small fortunes to obtain possession of a single coveted specimen.

This book is the first of its kind ever published, and contains illustrations of virtually every known variety of old silver spoon in existence.

It may be mentioned that the originals of many of the illustrations in this volume are valued at several hundred pounds apiece. It may be added, for the benefit of amateur collectors of small means, of whom the author is one, that others of the spoons here depicted cost only a few shillings each; but are not the less rare, beautiful, or interesting on that account.

The violet of many a legend blows about old silver spoons.

INTRODUCTION

Was it not a silver spoon which Henry VI left, together with his boots and gloves, at Bolton Hall, after the Battle of Hexham in 1445, although the supposed original has proved to be a later substitute?

Did not the silver Maidenhead spoons perpetuate for posterity the wondrous changes in the dress and coiffure of women of fashion in the fourteenth, fifteenth and sixteenth centuries?

Kings, queens, princes, nobles, and the wealthy, for centuries, carried folding spoons about with them on their travels, guests even taking their own when invited to a feast. Did not Queen Elizabeth in her "Progresses" carry one of these "foulden spones," made, in this case, of gold, about her person?

Were not a "wold silver spoon" and a "wold graven seal" the only tangible remnants of his distinguished descent possessed by the father of "Tess of the D'Urbervilles"?

References to silver spoons abound in literature from Shakespeare, Ben Jonson, and Beaumont and Fletcher, to Congreve, Butler, Ruskin and Carlyle.

Were not spoons used in the churches, in Tudor and pre-Tudor times, to strain the wine, receive the water for mixing with the wine, for taking the wafers out of the Ciborium, conveying the incense from the Navette to the Censer, and, almost within living memory, particularly in the North of England, as "In Memoriam" gifts to near relatives at a funeral? A York-made spoon of this latter sort is illustrated in this volume.

Was it not an engraved, two-piece, lobed-end, silver spoon, again, which Bonnie Prince Charlie carried with him, in a black shagreen case, during his five months' wanderings after the Battle of Culloden?

Authorities agree it is entirely likely that the Pilgrim Fathers numbered silver spoons, of the time of Elizabeth and James I, among their treasured possessions on the *Mayflower*.

INTRODUCTION

Was not the "spone" a favourite gift made to Henry VIII, as shown hereafter, "uppon Newe-yeres daye," by "the Ladie Marques Dorsett," "therle of Bridgewater," "the Lorde Marques of Excetor," and others of his nobles?

The silver spoon is a talisman. Who possesses even one need never want. For centuries it conferred distinction on its poorest owner. It was jealously preserved, handed down in wills and recorded in inventories. It is to this we owe largely the many beautiful specimens that still survive.

The saying is true in a dual sense that many a child is born with a silver spoon in its mouth, and the spoon is certainly one of the first things wanted in life, and one of the last parted with in death.

An ancient writer has pointed out that it proffers pap and teething material for the baby, porridge, soup, and puddings to the growing boy or girl, drives sickness away in the hands of the doctor, and solaces the last moments of millions.

Some even go so far as to contend that the fundamental difference in the respective habits and temper of the Saxon and Gaul may be found in the fact that the members of one race are essentially spoon-eaters, living on soups and stews, while the members of the other are the more carnivorous, habitual wielders of the knife and fork, the difference, in effect, between beef and *bouillon*, roast and *ragoût*.

Silver spoons have made their influence felt not once, but many times in the history and politics of the nation. They have been melted down, again and again, to make coins with which to pay soldiers in the wars, both international and civil.

The spoon, indeed, is bound up inseparably with the history of England from the sacred Incense Spoon of the ancient Church, the precious Anointing Spoon of Kings, and the Apostle and other silver spoons given

INTRODUCTION

at baptisms in the days of the Tudors and Stuarts, right down to the dainty specimens that chimed with the introduction of snuff and tea.

An early English Master Apostle Spoon, weighing only two or three ounces, fetches one hundred guineas and upwards, in the auction-room to-day, and American multi-millionaires, such as Mr. J. Pierpont Morgan, are proud to number a set of English Apostle spoons among their price-less art collections. There are " finds " always awaiting the collector, however, sometimes in the most unexpected places, at a relatively trifling cost.

Ancient spoons, unlike old furniture and old pictures, can be readily authenticated, their production and marking, like that of the coinage, having, for many centuries, been hedged round with drastic precautions and penalties, including, at one time, death.

They are inevitably growing scarcer, and, at the present relatively low prices, are bound to appreciate in value. The discriminating collector is not only able to indulge an absorbing hobby, but is, incidentally, making a very profitable investment against the future.

Few collectors are in a position to acquire, say, a complete set of twelve Apostle spoons with the Master. A set of these of the time of Henry VIII, weighing altogether less than thirty-three ounces, and worth in the melting-pot less than £5, realised £4,900 at Christie's in the early years of the present century, or nearly £150 an ounce.

A fascinating Provincial Lobed-end spoon of the time of Charles II, on the other hand, a small set of quaint caddy spoons, from George III to William IV, or a dozen delicious little Georgian teaspoons, are within reach of thousands of collectors of modest means.

An authentic, fully-marked dessert spoon, again, made possibly by a famous London woman silversmith of the time of George III, and

xii

INTRODUCTION

giving a lifetime's service of use and beauty, costs to-day little more than the price of a theatre seat.

I am indebted to Mr. Lionel Crichton, one of the greatest living authorities on the subject of ancient English silver spoons, and who has helped to form many of the famous private collections in this country, for permission to use the beautiful photographs of spoons from his own collection, now reproduced for the first time. The photographs are taken from Mr. Crichton's "case-book" of unusually fine, and, in many instances, historic spoons. I feel that no apology is needed for reproducing, unchanged, the excellent descriptions appended to each photograph as in the original case-book.

To the authorities at the Victoria and Albert Museum, South Kensington, I am greatly indebted for permission to use the photographs of a number of the wonderful spoons in the National Collection, and to Mr. H. W. Lewer, F.S.A., the editor of *The Collector Series*, for kindly reading the proof sheets of this book.

My thanks are further due to the Society of Antiquaries of London for its courtesy in allowing me to publish the list of spoons containe in Henry VIII's Jewel Book in the Society's library, to the Innholders' Company for permission to reproduce a photograph of one of its famous St. Julian spoons, and to the Mercers' Company for permission to give an illustration of its rare Hexagonal-top spoon, of which only two or three are known to-day.

The initials "L.C." appear with all photographs of spoons from Mr. Crichton's collection, and "V. & A.M." under photographs of spoons at South Kensington.

Amersham.   NORMAN GASK.

CONTENTS

ILLUSTRATIONS

B

xvii

ILLUSTRATIONS

OLD
SILVER SPOONS
OF ENGLAND

OLD SILVER SPOONS OF ENGLAND

CHAPTER I

THE FASCINATION OF OLD SILVER SPOONS

The added zest to food and drink—Collectors who carry old spoons on their
travels for personal use—The melting down of spoons for the Civil War—
Destruction in the Great Fire—Changing fashions also responsible—Ruskin
on the rich young couple's desire for new plate, and the magic of old
silversmiths' work—The Goldsmiths' Company's attempt to revive fine
hand-wrought silver.

IT was Juvenal who cited the belief that gold in contact with heat
emits a singularly sweet and fragrant odour, so that hot mulled
wine drunk from a golden chalice has an added savour.

Numbers of men and women to-day similarly declare that an old
silver spoon is not only a delight to the eye, but when used for
tea, coffee, soup, sweet or dessert, imparts an added zest to the food
or drink, and can be infallibly distinguished by the tongue or palate,
even with the eyes closed, from the most costly example of modern
silver plate. An old silver spoon, I am told, enhances particularly the
flavour of crushed strawberries.

I know, personally, of not a few instances in which men and
women carry one or two old silver spoons with them, for personal use,
on their travels at home or abroad, as did, many centuries ago, the

21

possessors of those famous Pre-Tudor Diamond-point folding spoons that are among the earliest silver spoons still in existence. A talented American woman writer of my acquaintance, who divides her time between England, Italy, and her home in California, carries her two favourite George III dessert spoons with her wherever she goes.

Wherein lies the extraordinary fascination of old silver spoons?

I have put the question, at various times, to a score or more enthusiastic collectors, and have received as many different replies.

Some praised the sparkling purity of the hand-wrought silver, which was probably smelted with charcoal instead of coal, declaring also that such silver had improved, like wine, with age. Others explained the fascination by the harmony and symmetry of the designs, conceived by great artists, and executed by famous craftsmen of the time.

Others, again, averred that old spoons, which were wrought for personal, individual use, possess more character and " atmosphere " than any other domestic silver made by a craft described as the noblest of all, the craft most favoured by kings and princes, and, indeed, practised, in ancient times, by some of the greatest in the land.

It is true that the founders of many of the peerages recorded in Burke's to-day were members of the ancient Goldsmiths' Company. It is true also that not only silversmith craftsmen, but architects, artists, sculptors, engravers and chemists, all contributed to the forging of a spoon.

Other collectors, again, found the fascination in the antiquarian interest of these veritable " inches of history," for, thanks to the researches of the late Octavius Morgan, Sir Charles Jackson, and others, into the question of date-letters and makers' marks, it is now possible to state not only the precise year and town in which, say, an

THE FASCINATION OF OLD SILVER SPOONS

Elizabethan Lion Sejant was made, but, as like as not, the name of the silversmith who made it, and something of the silversmith's personal career.

The melting down of ancient silver in the past to furnish the sinews of war, above all in the Civil War between King and Parliament, has undoubtedly contributed to the destruction of hosts of priceless examples of old silver spoons. The Great Fire of 1666 likewise took its toll of London-made specimens.

Changing fashion, however, must also be held to account for the thousands of beautiful and irreplaceable ancient spoons that have vanished into the melting pot.

Ruskin expresses himself with both force and point on the subject of " fashions " in silver, and the wanton destruction these have caused to shining examples of fine art and craftsmanship. His remarks apply equally to numbers of spoons, other than the Apostle spoons which he specifies as being retained.

" The first idea of a rich young couple setting up house in London is that they must have new plate," said Ruskin in discussing " The Political Economy of Art."

" Their father's plate may be very handsome, but the fashion is changed. They will have a new service from the leading manufacturer, and the old plate, except a few Apostle spoons, and a cup which Charles the Second drank a health in to their pretty ancestress, is sent to be melted down and made up with new flourishes and fresh lustre."

" Goldsmith's work," he continues, referring to both gold and silver ancient craftsmanship, " is made to last and made with the man's whole heart and soul in it ; true goldsmith's work, when it exists, is generally the means of education of the greatest painters and sculptors of the

23

OLD SILVER SPOONS OF ENGLAND

PLATE II

(1) Anglo-Saxon Spoon, the Original Found Near Barham, Kent. ? Fifth Century A.D. (From an Electrotype)

(2) The Coronation, or Anointing, Spoon. Front View. Date about 1200. Original in Tower of London. (From an Electrotype)

(3) Ancient Roman Spoon. Date about 500 A.D.

(4) Side View of Coronation Spoon.

[V. AND A. M.]

PLATE II

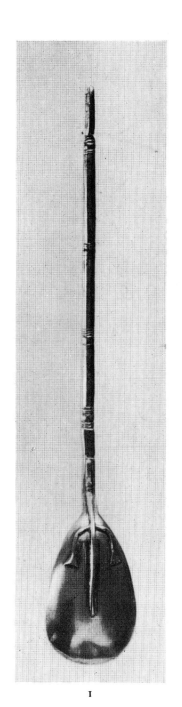

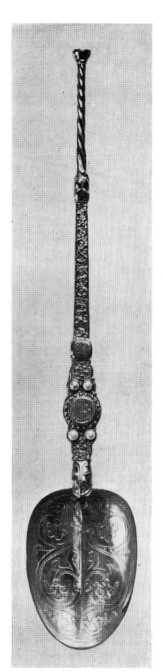

1

2

3

4

day. . . . You must keep it, though it should have the misfortune to become old-fashioned.

" You must not break it up nor melt it any more; there is no economy in that; you could not waste intellect more grievously. Nature may melt her goldsmith's work at every sunset if she chooses, and beat it out into chased bars again at every sunrise, but you must not.

" The way to have a truly noble service of plate is to keep adding to it, not melting it. At every marriage and at every birth get a new piece of silver if you will, but with noble workmanship on it, done for all time, and put it among your treasures.

" . . . When we know a little more of political economy," he adds, " we shall find none but partially savage nations need, imperatively, gold for their currency; but gold has been given us, among other things, that we might put beautiful work into its imperishable splendour, and that the artists who have the most wilful fancies may have a material which will drag out and beat out, as their dreams require, and will hold itself together with fantastic tenacity whatever rare and delicate service they set it upon."

Ruskin's words are particularly apposite to old silver spoons. The family whose ancestors since Tudor times had preserved specimens of the various sorts of silver and silver-gilt spoons, hand-wrought through the centuries, would possess not only a magnificent collection of beautiful forms of craftsmanship, but a treasure which museums and millionaires alike would envy.

Many of the wonderful forms of spoons made even in Tudor times, owing partly to changing fashion, are not in existence to-day, and can only be guessed at from their descriptions in the inventory of Henry VIII's Jewel House and elsewhere.

OLD SILVER SPOONS OF ENGLAND

It is not without significance that the Goldsmiths' Company is now making an attempt to restore the ancient traditions of the silversmith's craft, and to revive fine hand-wrought work in the precious metals in face of the opposing flood of machine-made wares. It is stated that so pressing has been the competition of spun and machine-produced work in gold and silver, that the craftsman, whose art reached its zenith in the magnificent creations of the sixteenth, seventeenth, and eighteenth centuries, has to-day been crushed out of existence.

CHAPTER II

THE SILVERSMITH TRADITION AND FAMOUS CRAFTSMEN

St. Dunstan, Alfred the Great, The Mediæval Monks, William of Wykeham, Holbein, the glory of Cheap in Tudor and Early Stuart times—List of the Goldsmith-Knights and Baronets.

IT is difficult to realise the atmosphere in which the early English silver spoons were wrought without knowing something of the early silversmiths and the traditions of the craft.

The list of official and unofficial silversmiths through the ages is an astonishing one. A new history of England could be written round their names.

The patron saint of English goldsmiths, and of the Goldsmiths' Company of London, is Saint Dunstan, born in 925 at Glastonbury. He is supposed to have learned the goldsmith's art in a monastery, which he entered when young, afterwards erecting near the famous Abbey of Glastonbury a cell which was both forge and oratory.

He employed part of his time here in making ecclesiastical vessels and ornaments, such as crosses and chalices, for the church, doing also general goldsmith's work for the clergy and laity alike.

King Edmund, the successor of the Saxon King Athelstan, made Dunstan Abbot of Glastonbury while he was still a young man, and he

27

became in turn Bishop of Worcester, Bishop of London, and, at the age of only twenty-four, Archbishop of Canterbury.

Some of Dunstan's handicraft was apparently in existence as late as A.D. 1280, 292 years after his death, the wardrobe accounts of Edward I recording " a gold ring with a sapphire, of the workmanship of St. Dunstan."

King Alfred the Great, again, encouraged, and it is believed actually supervised, the working of gold and silver into plate.

The King's friend and biographer describes how, when Alfred had obtained peace for his subjects, he decided to furnish them with a knowledge of the arts, and, to this end, assembled from many nations skilled workers in gold and silver, who, under his instructions, wrought with matchless skill numerous articles in these metals.

A rich, oval-shaped locket or brooch of gold, called the Alfred Jewel, and decorated with a portrait, believed to be that of the King himself, is still preserved in the Ashmolean Museum at Oxford.

It bears, round the bust, in Saxon characters, the words, " AELFRED MEC HEHT GEW(E)RCAN " (" Alfred had me made ") and was discovered by a ploughman in the reign of William and Mary, near the Abbey, in the Isle of Athelney, whither Alfred retreated in A.D. 878. It is reasonable to suppose that St. Dunstan and King Alfred designed spoons of either gold or silver, or both, although histcry is silent on this point. Silver spoons, made by the Romans centuries previously, have been unearthed in this country, and are still in existence.

Brithnodus, Abbot of Ely, was, in the twelfth century, a worker in gold and silver, and so was Robert, Abbot of St. Albans.

It was to these and other old monks that we owe much of the goldsmith's tradition, that passion for perfection, and delight in fine

OLD SILVER SPOONS OF ENGLAND

PLATE III

FIVE EARLY TREASURES AT SOUTH KENSINGTON

(1) MAIDENHEAD. LATE FOURTEENTH CENTURY. MARK — ARMS OF SEE OF COVENTRY.

(2) ACORN-KNOP. FIFTEENTH CENTURY. NO MARKS.

(3) THE FAMOUS WOODWOSE. EARLY LONDON HALL-MARK OF UNCROWNED LEOPARD'S HEAD WITHIN DOTTED CIRCLE OR RING OF PELLETS. POSSIBLY MADE AT COGGLESHALL, ESSEX, IN 1468.

(4) DIAMOND-POINT. LONDON, 1493–4. MAKER'S MARK, A FISH. DUG UP AT WANDSWORTH.

(5) LION SEJANT. FIFTEENTH CENTURY. LION SITTING SIDEWAYS. MARK, A CLOSED HELMET.

[V. AND A. M.]

PLATE IIı

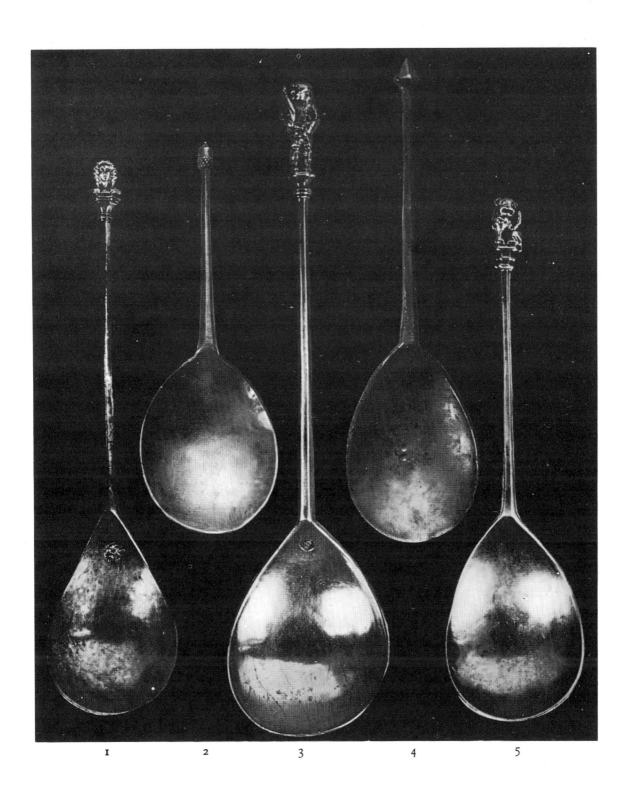

craftsmanship, which enabled the great art to survive centuries of wars, spoliations, and consignments of its products to the melting-pot to raise money, often for the wars.

No less than three tenants-in-chief under William the Conqueror are entered in Domesday Book under the title of "Aurifaber" (Goldsmith).

The great William of Wykeham, who was consecrated Bishop of Winchester in 1367, is said to have practised the goldsmith's art, and to have designed the celebrated Gothic crozier, which he bequeathed, with other plate, to New College, Oxford, of which he was the founder.

The silversmith's tradition was worthily maintained by Holbein, the great artist, who, in 1537, entered the service of Henry VIII, designing numerous pieces of goldsmith's work, including doubtless some of the marvellous spoons cited in the inventory of Henry's jewel-house described elsewhere in this book. The Ashmolean Museum possesses a drawing of a cup designed by Holbein for presentation to Jane Seymour.

Much of a rich man's wealth in former times, before the coming of the banks, was invested in wrought silver. Stocks and bonds, as we now understand them, had not been heard of in those far-off days.

The majority of the goldsmiths in the spacious days of Queen Elizabeth lived in "Cheap." Charles I, in order, partly, to impress foreigners with the wealth of the City, decreed that no establishments other than goldsmiths' should be situated in the City's great thoroughfare.

"At this time," wrote Rushworth, of the year 1629, "the City of London was in great splendour and full of wealth; and it was then a most glorious sight to behold the goldsmiths' shops all of one row in Cheapside, from the end of the street called Old Change, near Pater

SILVERSMITH TRADITION AND CRAFTSMEN

Noster Row, unto the open space over against Mercer's Chapel, at the lower end of Cheap, there being, at that time, but three or four shops of other trades that interposed in the Row."

A collector of to-day, if by means of some Time Machine he could be set down with a small, modern suit-case in the Cheapside of Charles' time, could, by the expenditure of only a few pounds, bring away sufficient spoons to maintain him in comfort, if need be, for life. He would concentrate, probably, on sets of Apostle, Maidenhead and Lion Sejant spoons, the earlier the better.

Paul de Lamerie, Paul Crespin, Thomas Harache, Hester Bateman, Eliza Godfrey, and a host of others, both men and women, maintained the fine tradition of the silversmith in the days of the Georges.

While spoonmaking was a specialised branch of the silversmith's art, many of the most famous silversmiths, whose names have come down to us, put their noted makers' marks on spoons.

The honour and repute in which the silversmith was held in ancient times, and the arts and crafts expected of him, are attested by the great roll of the goldsmiths and members of the Goldsmiths' Company. It will be observed that many of the names mentioned in the appended list are as familiar in the City banking and financial world of to-day as they were many centuries ago.

The close connection between these titled goldsmiths and the making of spoons is strikingly illustrated by a Master spoon in the J. H. Walter collection. This spoon, which bears the London Hall-mark and the rare Lombardic P. for 1492–3, has, for Maker's mark, the "touch" of none other than Sir Edmund Shaa, who was Warden of the Goldsmiths' Company, Master of the Mint, Cup Bearer and Goldsmith to Richard III, and in 1482 was elected Lord Mayor of London.

OLD SILVER SPOONS OF ENGLAND

These members of the Goldsmiths' Company, many of them acting in the capacity of bankers in the days when banks, as we now understand the term, did not exist, and the years in which the members are known to have been flourishing, include the following :—

EDWARD I
Sir William Faryngdon	1279
Sir Thomas de Frowick	1279

EDWARD II
Sir Nicholas Farengdon	1308
Sir Richard Britane	1326

EDWARD III
Sir John de Chichester	1359

RICHARD II
Sir Nicholas Twyford	1379
Sir Adam Bamme	1382
Sir John Frances	1390
Sir Drugo Barentyne (M.P. for City)	1394

HENRY VI
Sir John Pattisley	1432
Sir Matthew Phillips	1451
Sir Humphrey Hayford	1451
Sir Roger Brown	1451

EDWARD IV
Sir Edmund Shaa	1462
Sir Matthew Philip	1463
Sir Hugh Bryce	1469
Sir Humphrey Heyford	1477
Sir Bartholomew Reade	1481
Sir John Shaa	1483

HENRY VII
Sir Thomas Exmewe	1508

HENRY VIII
Sir Richard Martin	1509
Sir John Mundy	1509
Sir Roger Mundye	1518

SILVERSMITH TRADITION AND CRAFTSMEN

HENRY VIII (*continued*)

Sir John Thurston	1519
Sir Martin Bowes	1540
Sir John Williams	1540

EDWARD VI

Sir Thomas Gresham	1550

ELIZABETH

Sir John Langley	1567
Sir Hugh Myddleton	1600
Sir James Pemberton	1602

JAMES I

Sir William Ward	1609
Sir Thomas Exmewe	1618

CHARLES I

Sir John Wollaston	1638
Sir Thomas Viner or Vyner	1645

COMMONWEALTH

Sir George Viner	1658

CHARLES II

Sir Robert Viner	1662
Sir James Drax	1663
Sir Charles Doe	1666
Sir Jeremiah Snow	1668
Sir John Shorter	1668
Sir Thomas Cook	1670
Sir John Brattle	1670
Sir Richard Hoare	1672
Sir Thomas Fowles	1677

JAMES II

Sir Francis Child	1688

WILLIAM III

Sir Charles Duncombe	1700

ANNE

Sir Thomas Rawlinson	1707

GEORGE II

Sir Francis Gosling	1756

OLD SILVER SPOONS OF ENGLAND

PLATE IV

(1) DIAMOND-POINT. LONDON, FIFTEENTH CENTURY. MARK, UNCROWNED LEOPARD'S HEAD WITHIN DOTTED CIRCLE.

(2) GOTHIC FINIAL. DATE ABOUT 1500. [V. AND A. M.]

(3) THE FAMOUS ST. NICHOLAS SPOON, WHICH REALISED THE RECORD SUM OF £690 WHEN SOLD IN 1902. LONDON, 1528–9. MAKER'S MARK, ORB AND CROSS BETWEEN I.C. (JOHN CARSWELL). (FROM A SILVER FACSIMILE.) PHOTOGRAPH ABOUT TWO-THIRDS OF ACTUAL SIZE OF SPOON. [L.C.]

(4) APOSTLE, ST. JAMES THE GREATER. SECOND HALF OF FIFTEENTH CENTURY.

(5) WRYTHEN-KNOP. FROM THE AUTHOR'S COLLECTION. DATE, ABOUT 1500. SCOTTISH UNASCRIBED MARK. IB ? INVERNESS. [V. AND A. M.]

PLATE IV

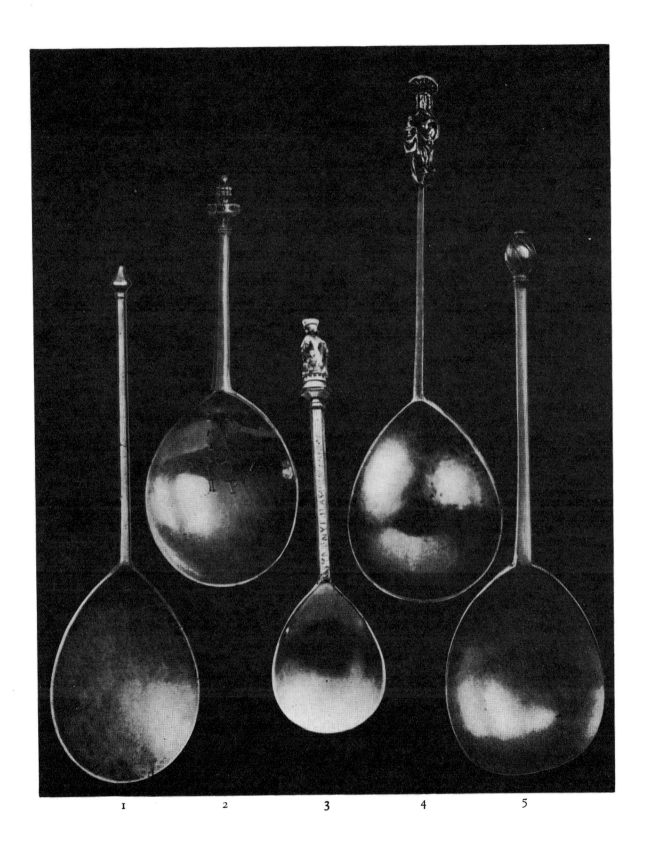

SILVERSMITH TRADITION AND CRAFTSMEN

Sir Thomas de Frowick, who was a warden of the Goldsmiths' Company, made the golden crown for the coronation of Edward Longshank's second Queen, Margaret, the daughter of Philip III of France.

Sir William Faryngdon gave his name to the City Ward of Faringdon, which name persists to-day. He purchased it in 1279, and it remained in his family for more than eighty years, the tenure being held by the annual presentation at Easter of a slip of "gilliflower," then a blossom of great scarcity.

Sir John de Chichester was a famous goldsmith in Edward III's time, his shop being at the corner of Friday Street, in the Chepe. He made the wedding jewellery for the King's son and the Lady Blanche.

Sir Martin Bowes was M.P. for London four times, from 1546 to 1555, and, incidentally, lent Henry VIII, who could not keep money, the sum of £300.

Sir Hugh Myddleton had his shop in Basinghall Street, an establishment much frequented by Sir Walter Raleigh.

Sir Hugh, who died in 1631, was one of London's greatest benefactors. He gave the metropolis its first pure water supply. His scheme for conveying a stream of water to London from St. Chad's springs, Ware, was carried out between 1609 and 1613. James I bore most of the expense, and took most of the profits, but granted the goldsmith a baronetcy without payment of the customary fee of £1,095.

It was Sir James Pemberton, who, being a Sheriff of London, at the proclamation of King James I, "entertained neere 40 erles and barons in his house."

Sir William Ward was jeweller to Charles I's Queen.

OLD SILVER SPOONS OF ENGLAND

Sir Thomas Viner, knighted by Cromwell, and created a baronet by Charles II, married Honor, the daughter of George Humble, the ancestor of Lord Dudley and Ward.

Sir Robert Viner, of Lombard Street, made the Crown Jewels for Charles II's coronation, at a cost of more than £30,000.

Says Pepys, under the date of February 1, 1666: "Thence to Sir Robert Viner's leaving clear in his hands £2,000 of my owne money, to call for when I pleased." Pepys recalls that Sir Robert, in a single transaction, cleared £10,000 by a timely loan to Charles II.

It was only in 1694 that the goldsmith-bankers met with a serious rival in the banking business by the foundation of the Bank of England.

CHAPTER III

THE FIRST SPOONS

The Shells of Fish the earliest Spoons—Cockle Shells of the Picts and Scots—Horn Spoons—Gold Spoons mentioned in Bible—Egyptian Spoons—Roman and Early Christian Silver Spoons—Bronze late Celtic Spoons—Horn, Wooden, Pewter, and Tinned-Iron Spoons of the Middle Ages—Latten Spoons.

IT may safely be asserted that spoons are of a very ancient pedigree, and, indeed, are almost as old as man himself.

The shells of fish were probably the earliest forms of all, and a shell as the spoon of the ancient inhabitants of Southern Europe is indicated by the Greek word *kochlias*, and the Latin word *cochlea*, meaning, respectively, snail and snail-shell. *Cochlearia* was the Roman word for spoons and this word was retained in mediæval wills and inventories. The Picts and Scots used cockle-shells.

Six " Sponez of welke shelles. . . . garneshed slightlie wt silver " are mentioned in the Jewel Book of Henry VIII, and the shell as a spoon still persists in remote country places as a caddy-spoon, a sugar spoon, or other similar utensil.

Some of the Scots, even to-day, drink whisky from shells, an ancient custom of their country, and many a London tobacconist, I believe, still reserves a shell for measuring out snuff.

37

OLD SILVER SPOONS OF ENGLAND

The negroes in Africa, the American Indians, the Arabs and Malays, continue to employ the most ancient form of spoon. This is a cleft stick, slipped over the edge of a shell, and then securely bound behind the joint with a thin sinew.

Horn was another material out of which both spoons and drinking vessels were made in remote times, and it is again significant that horn spoons are still considered by discerning housewives to be excellent utensils to use in mixing and serving salads.

Spoons of gold are specified, both in Exodus and the Book of Numbers, but no hint is given as to the form assumed by these Biblical varieties.

Egyptian spoons of slate, of flint, of wood and of ivory, are to be found in the British Museum.

Silver spoons of the Romans and Early Christians are also to be found in the British Museum. Some of them are characterised by long, almost spike-like, pointed stems, the points being used for opening shell-fish, extracting snails from their shells, and conveying the flesh to the mouth, much as the poorer Londoner of to-day eats whelks from a street barrow with the aid of a woman's hat-pin.

The pointed stems were also used, according to Pliny, for perforating eggs before eating them in order to ward off ill-effects.

Two comparatively small Roman silver spoons, found at Backworth, Northumberland, in 1812, with other treasure, including 290 coins, the latest of which was struck in A.D. 139, have pear or fig-shaped bowls, with the characteristic elbow at the junction of bowl and stem, as shown in the side view of the Anointing Spoon on Plate II, the third having a circular bowl, but all three the curious slender, bodkin-like stems.

38

THE FIRST SPOONS

The large later Roman silver spoon, also shown on Plate II, is similar to one found near Rose Lane, Canterbury, in 1868, and another discovered near an old bridge at Newcastle-on-Tyne.

The bowls, again, of some of the smaller Roman spoons found in England, are shaped like the shells of mussels. They are to be met with on rare occasions in the auction room or in the shops of dealers in antique silver.

The main feature of most of these, as of the early Christian spoons, is to be found in the manner in which the handle is united to the bowl. The bowl is not level with the stem, but underneath the bowl, and supporting it for half its length, is a sort of elbow. The bowl, when the stem is held in a horizontal position, is thus about half-an-inch below the stem.

Bronze Late-Celtic spoons, dating, perhaps, anywhere from 100–300 A.D., and consisting of small oval plates, slightly concave, have also been found in the Thames, and are thought to have been used by the early Christian Church for giving the Sacrament of Baptism.

All evidence concerning spoons between the end of the Roman dominion in Britain or the early Anglo-Saxon period, and the twelfth or thirteenth century, is largely conjecture.

The word " spoon " is derived from the Anglo-Saxon " spon " or chip, indicating that wood was the material of which the spoons of our Saxon ancestors were generally formed, horn and bone probably sharing the honour, however, in the Anglo-Saxon period. An electrotype of an Anglo-Saxon spoon, the original found near Barham, Kent, and attributed to the fifth century, is also shown on Plate II. Another Anglo-Saxon silver spoon, ornamented with garnets, the bowl perforated and washed with gold, was found in a grave at Chatham, and is now

39

in the Ashmolean Museum. A similar spoon has also been found in an Anglo-Saxon barrow at Stodmarsh, Kent.

Horn and wood seem to have been the favourite materials for everyday domestic use in the Middle Ages, silver spoons being used only in the homes of the rich, while gold spoons were the prerogative of the King.

Spoons of pewter, tinned-iron, and brass or latten were also common in the fourteenth and fifteenth centuries, and, when silver spoons were more generally introduced, they were faithfully copied in the baser metals.

CHAPTER IV

Early English, Rare and Famous Spoons

The Coronation or Anointing Spoon, the earliest English Silver Spoon known
to be in existence to-day—Acorn-knops, Diamond-points or Spearheads,
Maidenheads, Strawberry-knops, Wrythen or Fluted-Cone knops.

CORONATION SPOON

WHAT is the oldest English silver spoon known to be in
existence to-day?

Authorities seem to agree that it is the Coronation
Spoon, preserved among the Regalia in the Tower of London, and that
it has been most probably used in the Coronation of our monarchs since
the twelfth or early thirteenth century.

The spoon, which is 10¼ inches in length, and now weighs 3 oz. 8 dwts.,
is of silver-gilt, with four pearls in the broadest part of the handle, the
thin bowl, which is joined to the stem by a modified elbow, having a
beautiful arabesque pattern engraved on its surface.

The bowl, which is divided by a ridge down the middle into two
concave parts, is used to hold the oil for anointing the King or Queen.

A great controversy raged in the nineteenth century over the
question whether this spoon was the original Coronation spoon, or
whether the old spoon disappeared with the old Regalia of England in
the time of the Commonwealth, and a new spoon had been made for
the Coronation of Charles II after the Restoration.

EARLY, RARE AND FAMOUS SPOONS

The opinion that it was a late seventeenth century spoon was largely prompted by the discovery of a document dated February 23rd, 1684, containing, in a list of Regalia for Charles II's Coronation, the item, " the anointing spoon, poiz 3 oz. 5 dwts. . . . for silver and workmanship . . . £2." It is now believed that this small sum of £2 referred to another spoon, or merely to repairs to the more ancient spoon.

It has been suggested that the Coronation Spoon may have been made originally as a chalice spoon in the early thirteenth century for use at the Coronation of Henry III, for whom new regalia had to be made because of the loss of the old Crown Jewels by King John while crossing the Wash. (Illustrations on Plate II.)

ACORN-KNOPS

The glass cases at Christie's, displaying ancient silver about to come under the hammer, sometimes contain a smallish silver spoon, midway in size between the modern teaspoon and the modern dessert-spoon. The unpretentious little spoon has a fig- or pear-shaped bowl and a slender handle, which is either four-sided and called " diamond section," or else somewhat rounded and bodkin-like, topped by a silver acorn.

This spoon, for all its sparkling brightness and appearance of having been just manufactured by a West End silversmith, is probably more than 400 years old, one of the famous Acorn-knops, and the first definite type of old English spoon of which we have any authentic record.

It is carried round in a tilted tray for the inspection of dealers and private collectors at the auction a day or two afterwards, and is then knocked down, if it is a later specimen and unmarked, for, say, £8 10s.,

OLD SILVER SPOONS OF ENGLAND

PLATE V

FIFTEENTH CENTURY

DIAMOND-POINTS AND MAIDENHEADS
SHOWING UNCROWNED LEOPARD'S HEADS IN DOTTED CIRCLES

OFFICE	COUNTERMARK	MAKER	LETTER	DATE	INITIALS &c.
	NIL	NIL	NIL	XV CENTY	

Spoon, pear shaped bowl, slender hexagonal stem with pointed knob.

LEOPARD'S HEAD (IN ROUND PUNCH)	NIL	NIL	NIL	XV CENTY	

Spoon, pear shaped bowl, slender hexagonal stem with pointed knob.

LEOPARD'S HEAD (IN ROUND PUNCH)	NIL	NIL	NIL	CIRCA 1480	

Spoon, pear shaped bowl, hexagonal stem surmounted by a maiden's head.

[L.C.]

PLATE V

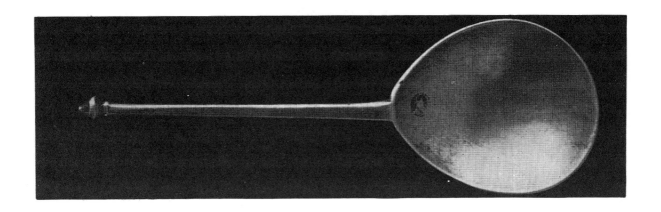

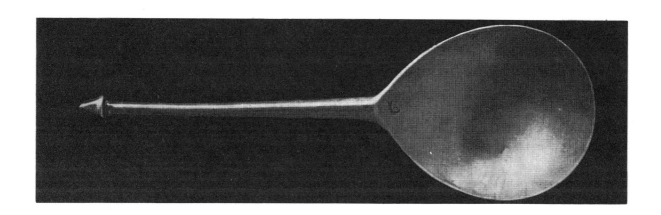

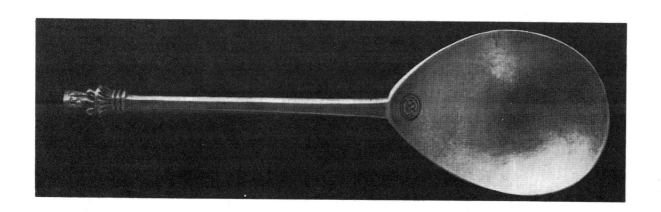

as was the case at the McQuoid sale in 1925, or it realises perhaps three or four times that sum, according to its age, condition, marks, pedigree, and a dozen other qualifying circumstances.

One of the first references that can be traced to this form of spoon is to be found in a will of 1348, proved at the Court of Husting, London, in 1351, whereby John de Holegh bequeathed to Thomas Taillour twelve silver spoons with " akernes." The records of the same Court also show that John Botiller, draper, in a will, dated 1361, bequeathed to Isabella, his wife, twelve best spoons with gilt acorns.

Six silver spoons, " cum acrinsse de auro," are likewise mentioned in a will dated 1392, registered at York, and these were, no doubt, spoons with gilt knops or heads shaped like acorns.

Similar spoons, described as " Dim. Dos Coclearium cum Akehornes," are also mentioned in a will dated 1459.

The will of the Countess of Northumberland, filed in 1542, specifically mentions in her bequests, " a spone with an acorne doble gilt."

These are the first references that can be discovered to English silver spoons of a more or less definite variety.

A dozen silver spoons, " Coclearia Argenti," are certainly mentioned in the will of Martin de St. Cross, a will dated as early as 1259, but there is no mention of their shape.

The same statement applies to an entry in the wardrobe accounts of Edward I, of the year 1300, which refers to seven gold, and eight silver spoons, marked in the stem with the fleur-de-lis, the " touch " of Paris, indicating that they came from France. An inventory of the Crown Jewels of Edward III, made in the year 1329, likewise mentions thirty-six silver spoons, plain white, stamped with the leopard, and five spoons of gold; but again there is no indication of their shape.

EARLY, RARE AND FAMOUS SPOONS

The Acorn-knop appears to have been a great favourite in the fifteenth century. The image of the acorn on spoons of this period is often very small, sixteenth century spoons generally, but not always, showing not only a considerably larger acorn, but a stouter stem and a longer bowl.

The Acorn-knop, then, came in about the fourteenth century, and lasted until late in the sixteenth. A good Elizabethan example, with a hexagonal shaft or stele tapering to the top, showing the date letter of 1593, the maker's mark, a crescent enclosing a mullet, in a plain circle, sold at public auction for £34 in 1902. A fifteenth century Acorn-knop realised £29 in 1907.

These spoons rarely find their way into the market to-day. A fine long-stemmed specimen dug up at Coventry, and ascribed to about the year 1400, and another, with a considerably shorter stem and a smaller acorn, attributed to the fifteenth century, are in the national collection at South Kensington.

They are shown respectively on Plates XXV and III. An Acorn-knop acquired by Mr. Crichton, and ascribed to 1470–1500, had the Crowned X, the famous town-mark of Exeter, punched on the front of the stem near the bowl.

DIAMOND-POINTS OR SPEARHEADS

Another variety of late fourteenth, fifteenth and sixteenth century spoon, is that which has its shaft terminating in an hexagonal spearhead or diamond-point.

These spoons were popular in the fifteenth and early sixteenth centuries, when their manufacture was discontinued. A silver Diamond-point hinged, or folding, spoon, found in a grave in St. Mary's Church,

45

Scarborough, and now belonging to the Scarborough Archæological Society, is assigned to the fourteenth century.

The items, " ij dosen and vj sponys with dyamond poyntes," are mentioned in an inventory now in the British Museum, of Robert Morton, gentleman, of the year 1487.

A Diamond-point in the J. H. Walter collection is marked with the uncrowned Leopard's Head within a dotted circle, and is ascribed to about the year 1400, and a similar one in the Lord Hylton collection to about 1450.

Beautiful fifteenth century specimens are shown on Plates IV, V and VI. Another, dug up at Wandsworth, bearing the London marks for 1493-4, with the maker's mark, a fish, is now at South Kensington, and is shown on Plate III.

Seven spoons with " dyamond poynts," bearing the London marks for 1565-6, and with " R.K." over a mullet or star as the maker's mark, are in the possession of the Mercers' Company of London.

A Diamond-point of the fifteenth century, with a hexagonal shaft tapering towards the end, and marked inside the bowl with the uncrowned Leopard's Head in a dotted circle, the earliest known London hall-mark, fetched £29 in 1904. A similar spoon, in good condition, would realise considerably more than that sum to-day.

More than one Diamond-point has been fished out of the Thames.

MAIDENHEADS

A close rival in point of age to the Acorn-knop and Diamond-point is the Maidenhead, that is, a spoon with the head and bust, supposed to represent the Virgin Mary, at the top of the handle. An unusually early example of this variety of spoon, with a gilt image of the Virgin, is to be seen at the Victoria and Albert Museum.

This is a comparatively small spoon with a very narrow pear-shaped bowl, which appears almost to have been cut away at the sides, a long, very narrow neck, and a long, slender, four-sided diamond-section stem. It is stamped clearly in the bowl with the arms of the See of Coventry. This mark seems closely to resemble the cross, which appears on Mediæval short-cross silver pennies, with a cross-piece at the end of each of the four arms of the cross, and a small cross in each of the four angles.

It comes from the famous H. D. Ellis collection. It is ascribed by the Museum authorities to the fourteenth century, which would make it one of the earliest English silver spoons in existence. It is shown on Plate III.

Sketches of the side view of a Henry VIII Maidenhead from the Author's collection, and of the detail of the beautiful gilt knop, are here shown.

The first published record referring to Maidenheads is an inventory of Durham Priory, of the year 1446, which mentions, " ij coclearia argentea et deaurata, unius sectae, cum ymaginibus Beatae Mariae in fine eorundem."

Three spoons, " wt womens heddes and faces," are mentioned in Henry VIII's Jewel Book.

An inventory of the worldly goods of Dame Agnes Hungerford, dated 1523, refers to " halfe a dossen of sylver spounys with mayden heedes on the end, gylte," a 1575 inventory of Archbishop Parker to " xij spones, withe mayden heddes," and another

OLD SILVER SPOONS OF ENGLAND

PLATE VI

FIFTEENTH CENTURY

WRYTHEN-KNOP, APOSTLE ST. ANDREW, AND DIAMOND-POINT

HALL	STANDARD	MAKER	LETTER	DATE	INITIALS &c
LEOPARD'S HEAD CROWNED (IN ROUND PUNCH)	NONE			1488	

Spoon, pear shaped bowl, slender hexagonal stem with spirally fluted knob.

HALL	STANDARD	MAKER	LETTER	DATE	INITIALS &c
LEOPARD'S HEAD CROWNED (IN ROUND PUNCH)	NONE			1490	

Apostle spoon, St. Andrew with a cross, plain nimbus, hexagonal stem, pear shaped bowl.

HALL	STANDARD	MAKER	LETTER	DATE	INITIALS &c
LEOPARD'S HEAD CROWNED (IN ROUND PUNCH)	NONE			1490	

Spoon, pear shaped bowl, slender hexagonal stem and pointed knob.

[L.C.]

PLATE VI

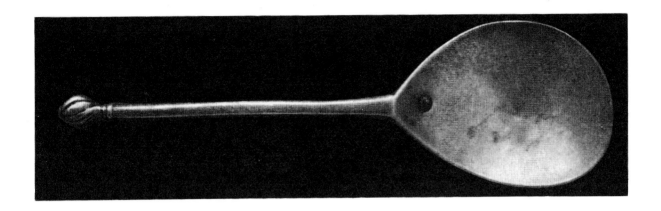

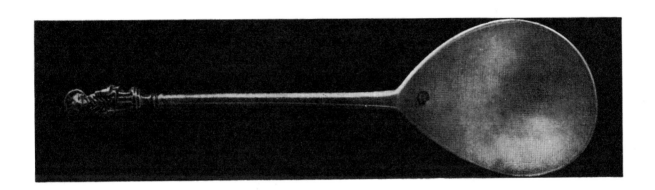

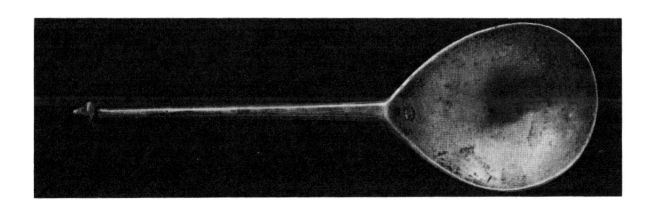

EARLY, RARE AND FAMOUS SPOONS

inventory of 1525 to a " spone knopped with the image of our lady."

Maidenhead spoons frequently show the approximate dates at which they were made by the manner in which the hair is dressed, and the drapery on the bust of the little image at the top of the spoon.

The earliest late fourteenth century examples show the moderate horned head-dress of the period, and those of Henry V the extreme and more pointed horns.

Fashion is more or less faithfully reflected in the head and bust of Our Lady right up to the latter part of the sixteenth century.

A silver Maidenhead of about the year 1400 is in the Sir Charles Jackson collection, and one of about 1450, with a long, narrow bowl, in the George Dunn collection.

A beautiful small Maidenhead in the King Edward wing of the British Museum bears the London marks for 1523–4.

The making of Maidenhead spoons continued until the time of James I. They are much sought after by collectors, and realise anywhere from £30 to £75 apiece, according to marks, age and condition.

A London Maidenhead of 1487, for instance, with the maker's mark, a wheel, realised £46 in 1903. A Maidenhead of the time of Henry VIII, dated 1528, again fetched £78 in 1909, and an Elizabethan example £72 in the preceding year. A James I Maidenhead of 1609–10, with a D enclosing C, as the maker's mark, sold for thirty guineas at the Breadalbane sale in May, 1926.

Other illustrations on Plates V, XII and XIV.

49

OLD SILVER SPOONS OF ENGLAND

STRAWBERRY-KNOPS

Other early English silver spoons are what are known as Strawberry-knops or Fruitlet-knops, that is, spoons with the shaft topped by a strawberry, bunch of grapes or other fruit.

Six silver spoons, " de Fradelett," are mentioned in a will of the year 1440, and six others, " cum Fretlettez," in an entry fifty years later.

These spoons are essentially fifteenth century productions, and are so rare as to be practically unknown in the auction room.

Six " gilt spones with strawbery knoppes " are mentioned in an inventory of the Merchant Taylors' Company of London, dated 1512.

WRYTHEN-KNOPS

Wrythen-knops, with the head composed of a ball or cone, fluted or spirally twisted, are another form of early Tudor or late pre-Tudor spoons that, on very rare occasions, find their way into the market, where they command prices up to 100 guineas apiece.

Robert Morton's inventory of 1487 mentions, " Ij dosen spones with wrethyn knoppes." Six " gilt spones with wrethen knoppes " are mentioned in the 1512 inventory of the Merchant Taylors' Company.

A Wrythen-knop of 1488–9, with the marker's mark, a wheel, realised 100 guineas at the Breadalbane sale in May, 1926.

A beautiful example of the same year, with a key as its maker's mark, is shown on Plate VI.

Another Wrythen-knop from the Author's collection, once the property of the Marquis of Breadalbane and now at South Kensington,

50

EARLY, RARE AND FAMOUS SPOONS

bears, as its only mark, the capital letters I B beneath a pellet, the whole within a dotted circle, punched in the bowl of the spoon. It is of Scottish origin, ascribed to about the year 1500, the I B being possibly an ancient Inverness mark. It is illustrated on Plate IV.

Wrythen-knops (from the Anglo-Saxon word " writhe," meaning twisted) appear to have gone out of fashion early in the sixteenth century. Only a few are known to be in existence to-day.

CHAPTER V

EARLY, RARE AND FAMOUS SPOONS (*Continued*)

The St. Nicholas, the Woodwose, Terminal-Figure knops including the famous late Elizabethan set of twelve Celebrities—Falcon-knops, Doves or Columbynes, Square-knops, Hexagonals or Six-Squared-knops, Owl-knops, Ball-knops, Angel-knops, Finials, Scallop-Shell-knops, Sickle-knops, Mitre-knops, Horse-Hoof-knops, Folding Spoons.

ST. NICHOLAS

THE St. Nicholas spoon, which came from the famous Dunn-Gardner collection, has the distinction of realising the highest sum ever paid for a single spoon. It is an unusually fine spoon, partly gilt. The stem, which is of the usual flattened hexagonal section, is inscribed " Synt Nycolas, pray for ws " in Roman capitals, and is surmounted by the figure of St. Nicholas restoring to life the children in the tub. St. Nicholas, who lived in the fourth century, was Bishop of Myra, and was known as the special protector of children. The Bishop, on one occasion, during a famine, so the legend runs, missed three of his boy pupils, and traced them to an inn, where he found them cut up and in process of being pickled in a brine-tub. He took them out, adds the legend, and restored them to life. The spoon bears the London hall-mark and date-letter for 1528–9, with the orb and cross between the initials I. C. (John

OLD SILVER SPOONS OF ENGLAND

PLATE VII

LATE FIFTEENTH AND EARLY SIXTEENTH CENTURY

APOSTLE ST. PAUL, SLIPPED-IN-THE-STALK AND MASTER

HALL	STANDARD	MAKER	LETTER	DATE	INITIALS &c
LEOPARD'S HEAD CROWNED (IN ROUND PUNCH)	NONE			1493	

Apostle spoon, St. Paul with a sword and a bowl, on his back hangs a round object like a cap suspended from the shoulders, a pierced nimbus on his head, hexagonal stem, pear shaped bowl. — A very fine example —

LEOPARD'S HEAD CROWNED (IN ROUND PUNCH)	NONE	ILLEGIBLE		1500	

Spoon, pear shaped bowl, hexagonal stem cut off obliquely at the end. — The date letter is at the extreme end of stem. —

LEOPARD'S HEAD CROWNED (IN ROUND PUNCH)	NONE			1514	

Spoon with gilt statuette of The Saviour with an orb & cross and hand raised in benediction, a dove in relief on the nimbus, hexagonal stem, pear shaped bowl. — A fine example. —

[L.C.]

PLATE VII

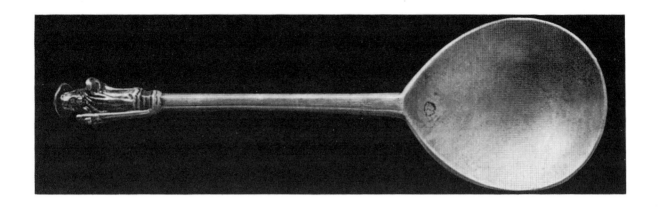

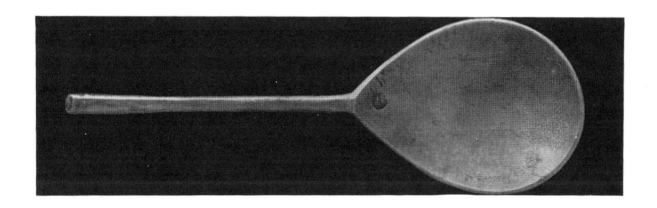

Carswell) as the maker's mark. It caused considerable excitement at the sale at Christie's in 1902, when it finally realised the sum of £690.

This spoon is said to have been used in the Abbey of St. Nicholas, Abingdon.

A rough sketch of the knop, designed, principally, to show the children in the tub, is presented herewith. An illustration of a silver facsimile of the spoon appears on Plate IV.

ST. JULIAN

A Henry VIII spoon, knopped with the figure of St. Julian, with the London date-letter for 1539–40, and, for maker's mark, the famous fringed " S," was exhibited by the Worshipful Company of Innholders at the Victoria and Albert Museum in the summer of 1926.

St. Julian, the Herberger or Keeper, was reputed to have lived in the fourth century, and is the patron saint of the Innholders' Company. He was an elderly man when he assumed the rôle of " Herbergeour," and the beautiful knop of this spoon accordingly represents a man with a flowing beard.

The Company possesses no fewer than twenty-three of these wonderful spoons, which cost only a few shillings apiece at the time they were made during various reigns, but are to-day worth a small fortune.

The early examples were probably provided by members for their own use, but in 1657 the gift of a spoon to the Company by each member was made compulsory. Specimens of the time of Henry VIII, Elizabeth, James I, Charles I, and Cromwell, are all included in the Company's collection.

54

EARLY, RARE AND FAMOUS SPOONS

I am indebted to the Innholders' Company for permission to reproduce the photograph of the Henry VIII example shown on Plate X.

WOODWOSE-KNOP

This is an extremely rare fifteenth century spoon, of which only one example, that in the Victoria and Albert Museum, is known to be in existence to-day.

Woodwose means a wild-man or mad-man, " wode " being early English for wild or mad, and " wose " signifying a being.

This remarkable spoon, which is from the H. D. Ellis collection, carries an image of a wild man in skins holding a club, at the top of the shaft.   It bears the early London hall-mark, but was possibly made at Coggleshall, Essex, in 1468.   Mr. Ellis has pointed out that in the minutes of the Goldsmiths' Company of London, under the date just mentioned, it is recorded that the Wardens of the Company, on one of their tours of inspection, journeyed to Coggleshall, and there examined a dozen silver spoons " with woodwoses," suspected of having been improperly stamped with the London hall-mark, the " Liberd's Heed " (Leopard's Head).

The Wardens found the spoons in the possession of one, John Fabian, of Coggleshall, seized them on suspicion of being below standard, and proved them to contain an excess of alloy.

Fabian, in his defence, declared the spoons had been made by one Deryk Knyff, who admitted the truth of this assertion, but said that he, in turn, had bought the metal from one, Thomas Coundrey, although he, Knyff, had added the finials or knops.

The Wardens found Knyff and Coundrey guilty, imposed suitable fines, ordered the spoons to be destroyed, and issued instructions that

55

OLD SILVER SPOONS OF ENGLAND

Knyff and Coundrey should supply to Fabian a dozen similar spoons of full standard purity.

A fifteenth century spoon, sold at Christie's in 1900, by order of the executors of "a deceased gentleman" in East Anglia, in whose family it had been for generations, was described in the catalogue as having at the top of the handle "a chased figure of a man in skin raiment, holding a club," and marked with the early Leopard's Head.

This is the spoon at South Kensington, and Mr. Ellis conjectures it was one of the spoons mentioned in the record of the Wardens' visit to Coggleshall.

A will was also proved at York in 1486, in which the testatrix bequeathed "sex cochlearia argenti cum wodwysshes deauratis," and again, the will of Agnes Hildyard, proved in 1498, bequeathed "sex cochlearia optima arg. cum wodwoshes."

TERMINAL FIGURES

These are spoons knopped with figures which do not fall within the usual categories, such as the seated figure of the Virgin, Krishna, a greyhound, or other image. Strictly speaking, the St. Julian, St. Nicholas, and the Woodwose are Terminal Figure spoons.

A set of twelve of these, known as the Tichborne family series, the property of Sir Joseph Tichborne, Bart., and one of the most remarkable sets of silver-gilt Tudor spoons ever made, sold at Christie's, in June, 1914, for the sum of £2,000. This amount, although it is eclipsed by the £4,900 paid for the set of twelve Henry VIII Apostles and the Master, is one of the highest figures ever reached for a set of silver

EARLY, RARE AND FAMOUS SPOONS

spoons. The series, the only one of its kind known to be in existence, is dated 1592–3, and is known as the " Celebrities " set. The maker's mark, a Crescent enclosing W., the whole in a shaped shield, is here shown.

The silversmith who designed them, having fashioned a Master spoon, and one Apostle spoon—St. Peter—broke away from all conventional traditions. The figures in which the handles of the twelve terminate are, as shown by the names clearly and beautifully engraved on the fronts of the handles, made up as follows :—

> The Saviour or Master
> St. Peter
> King David
> Judas Maccabeus
> Joshua
> Alexander the Great
> Charlemagne ("Charolus Magnus")
> Hector of Troy
> Julius Cæsar
> King Arthur
> Guy of Warwick
> Queen Elizabeth

It is surmised that the silversmith made a thirteenth spoon knopped with the figure of Henry VIII, but this is pure conjecture.

I am indebted to Mr. Crichton for the photograph of this unique set shown on the frontispiece.

The famous Terminal Figure spoon, known as the Krishna or Buddha knop, is described under " Unascribed Marks " in the Provincial section.

OLD SILVER SPOONS OF ENGLAND

FALCON-KNOPS AND DOVE-KNOPS

Spoons knopped with falcons or with doves (" columbynes ") are rare mediæval examples mentioned in Henry VIII's Jewel Book and elsewhere, of which virtually none has survived.

SQUARE-KNOPS

These were a further ancient form of spoon mentioned in wills, inventories and the same Jewel Book, although it is difficult to describe their precise appearance as, again, none apparently is in existence.

HEXAGONALS OR SIX-SQUARED KNOPS

Another very rare, but, at all events existing, spoon is the Hexagonal or " Six-squared knop," with a head not unlike a crown.

One of these was shown at an exhibition of silver plate at the Burlington Fine Arts Club, from the collection of Mr. R. E. Brandt. It bore the date-letter for 1480–1. This variety ceased to be made after Tudor Times.

Only two or three of these spoons are known to be in existence to-day.

One of them, formerly belonging to Whittington College, and now in the possession of the Worshipful Company of Mercers, caused great interest when it was shown at the London Livery Companies' Exhibition, held at the Victoria and Albert Museum in the summer of 1926.

This was an early Elizabethan specimen, bearing the London Hall-Marks for 1565–6, despite the fact that it appeared to be almost pin-new.

EARLY, RARE AND FAMOUS SPOONS

The Maker's Mark was R.K. above a mullet or star, showing that the spoon was made by the same maker in the same year as the seven Diamond-points, already described as in the Mercers' Company's possession.

The knop of this spoon was roughly the shape and size of a small gooseberry, coming to a point at the extreme top, with six pointed leaf-shaped sides, however, modifying the roundness of the surface—hence the name "Six-squared."

An illustration of this rare spoon is shown on Plate XIII by courtesy of the Mercers' Company. A number of "Six-squared" spoons are recorded in the Jewel Book of Henry VIII.

OWL-KNOPS AND BALL-KNOPS

Among the other varieties of spoons that, so far as the collector is concerned, have ceased to exist, may be mentioned Bishop Oldham's six spoons, with owls at the end of their stems, of the year 1506–7, and Bishop Fox's six, with gilt balls, of the year 1516–17, all twelve now carefully preserved at Corpus Christi College, Oxford.

ANGEL-KNOPS

A will of the year 1546 mentions " Ij sylver sponys withe angells on the knoppys gyltyd." Henry VIII possessed examples of this spoon as his Jewel Book shows.

FINIALS

These rare varieties, which belong to the fourteenth, fifteenth and sixteenth centuries, are spoons knopped with the small spike, spire,

OLD SILVER SPOONS OF ENGLAND

PLATE VIII

SLIPPED-IN-THE-STALKS AND APOSTLE ST. BARTHOLOMEW

EARLY HENRY VIII. SHOWING FAMOUS FRINGED "S" MAKER'S MARK

HALL	STANDARD	MAKER	LETTER	DATE	INITIALS &c
LEOPARD'S HEAD CROWNED (IN ROUND PUNCH)	NONE			1515	

Spoon, hexagonal stem cut off obliquely at the end, pear shaped bowl.

HALL	STANDARD	MAKER	LETTER	DATE	INITIALS &c
LEOPARD'S HEAD CROWNED (IN ROUND PUNCH)	NONE			1519	

Spoon, pear shaped bowl, hexagonal stem, cut off obliquely at the end.

HALL	STANDARD	MAKER	LETTER	DATE	INITIALS &c
LEOPARD'S HEAD CROWNED (IN ROUND PUNCH)	NONE			1519	

— One of a set from the Bernal Collection. —
St. Bartholomew with a knife & a book. A gilt Apostle spoon, pear shaped bowl, hexagonal stem, the nimbus having a star of eight rays.

[L.C.]

PLATE VIII

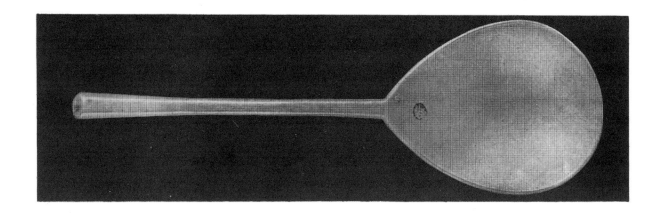

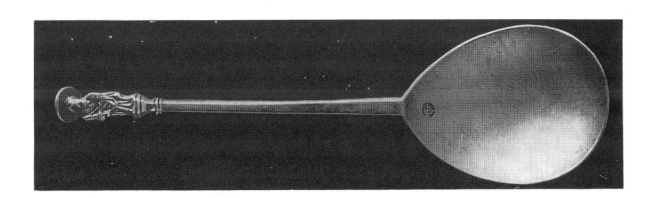

or other terminal ornamentation, which graces Gothic or other architecture.

A beautiful example of a silver parcel-gilt spoon with a Gothic Finial, and ascribed to about the year 1500, has recently been acquired by the Victoria and Albert Museum.

It belonged to the Postlethwayt family, of Millom, Cumberland, and is inscribed in the bowl with the initials of five generations of the family. It is shown on Plate IV.

A spoon with a hexagonal finial, acquired by Mr. Crichton, bore the date-letter for 1494–5, with W. or a double V. in an outline shield as the maker's mark. Another Finial obtained by him was dated 1532–3, with a sort of inverted curved V in a plain shield as the maker's symbol.

A York example, assigned to between the years 1490 and 1500, is described in the " Provincial Spoons " section.

Two finial-tops with unascribed marks, acquired by Mr. Crichton, and assigned to the 1570–80 period, had as their only marks a sort of seeded rose in a circle of pellets, and the letters P D in a plain rectangular shield.

SCALLOP-SHELL KNOPS

Wills and inventories from the Registry of the Archdeaconry of Richmond mention under date of 1558 " XII silver spones wt skallap shells on their heads. . . . "

SICKLE-KNOPS

An inventory, dated 1523, of the personal effects of Dame Agnes Hungerford mentions " iij dossen of sylver sponys with knottes of sykyls

OLD SILVER SPOONS OF ENGLAND

on the hed," the sickle being a badge of Hungerford. Sickle-knops are also itemised in the inventory of the spoons in Henry VIII's Jewel House.

MITRE-KNOPS

An inventory of Minster Priory, Sheppey, Kent, dated 1536, mentions "a dosen of sylver spones with myters, the myters beyng gilt."

HORSE-HOOF KNOPS

These rare seventeenth century spoons, which were used for medicine, are knopped with the hoof of a horse, showing a well-defined shoe on the hoof. There is an ornamental shoulder at the bottom of the shaft. A silver Horse-hoof knop, bearing the date-letter for 1652–3, was exhibited by Dr. Lloyd Roberts, at the Burlington Fine Arts Club, in 1901. Another specimen of an earlier date was sold a few months ago for about £40. An illustration of a small late example appears on Plate XXVIII.

FOLDING-SPOONS

Folding-spoons, already referred to, are also of ancient lineage. Examples of these spoons appear to be indicated in a York inventory of 1410 referring to " de uno Cocliari Plexibili," and an entry of 1432 citing " unum coclear argenti falden." A reference to " my foulden sylver spoone " appears in another inventory of the fifteenth century.

An early Georgian Folding-spoon in the Author's collection, with a silver rat-tail bowl, and a handle of horn bound with brass, is shown on Plate XXVI.

CHAPTER VI

APOSTLE SPOONS

Apostles, the most popular Spoons in Tudor times and the most eagerly sought after by collectors to-day—References to Apostle Spoons by Ben Jonson, Beaumont and Fletcher and Shakespeare—When introduced—Earliest known specimen now in existence—Complete set Twelve Apostles and a Master—Set of fourteen including Maidenhead, now unknown—Apostle Spoons used for Christenings—Tudor child's first taste of religion—Social distinction conferred by possession of even one spoon—How the twelve Apostles may be distinguished—Missing emblems—The record price of £4,900 for a complete set—Details of the set and sale—The maker's mark on this set—One Thousand Guineas for two spoons—Other prices—The set of eight at Breadalbane sale—The mysterious maker's mark of the Fringed Letter S.

THE Apostle was probably the most popular spoon of the Tudor period, as it is also the ancient spoon most eagerly sought after by collectors to-day. These varieties were variously described in Tudor times as " spones with appostells," " postle spones " and " appostell spons," and frequent references to them are found in literature of the Tudor and Stuart periods.

Ben Jonson, for example, in his *Bartholomew Fair*, makes one of his characters say, " All this for the hope of two Apostle spoons and a cup to eat caudle in."

Beaumont and Fletcher's *Noble Gentleman* also contains the lines :

> " I'll be a gossip, Bewford,
> I have an odd Apostle-spoon."

OLD SILVER SPOONS OF ENGLAND

Both Master and Apostle spoons are mentioned in Henry VIII's Jewel Book.

These remarkable spoons, which originated on the Continent, were introduced into England, it is believed, about the year 1450, although no record of them in wills and inventories has yet been discovered earlier than 1494, when " XIIJ (13) cocliaria argenti cum Apostolis super eorum fines " are found to have been bequeathed by a will in the York Registry.

The earliest definitely known specimen, until a few years ago, bore the London date-letter for 1490–1. An Apostle acquired by Mr. Crichton in 1920, however, which had the Leopard's Head crowned within a circular shield, with the initials N I above a Pellet, also in a circular shield, as the Maker's Mark, bore the Lombardic style letter A, indicating that it was made in 1478–9, in the reign of Edward IV.

This A. has hitherto been one of the missing letters in the first Lombardic alphabet covering the 1478–1497 period, the Lombardic B. having been heretofore the earliest letter of the cycle found stamped on any piece of plate.

These spoons continued to be made right up to Commonwealth times. Examples as late as the reign of William and Mary are sometimes seen, and even early Georgian specimens—probably made to complete a set of which one spoon had been lost—are encountered, but neither of these tardy specimens is taken seriously by collectors.

The spoons were so named because each is surmounted by a little silver-gilt figure of one of the Apostles bearing his customary emblem.

A complete set numbered thirteen spoons—that is, twelve Apostle spoons and a Master spoon bearing an image of Christ.

There were even, it is stated, sets of fourteen spoons, such sets having as the extra unit a Lady spoon or Maidenhead, bearing the head

OLD SILVER SPOONS OF ENGLAND

PLATE IX

APOSTLES: ST. PETER, ST. JAMES THE GREATER, AND ST. PHILIP

EARLY HENRY VIII. SHOWING FRINGED "S" MAKER'S MARK

HALL	STANDARD	MAKER	LETTER	DATE	INITIALS &c
LEOPARD'S HEAD CROWNED (IN ROUND PUNCH)	NONE			1519	

— *One of a set from the Bernal Collection.* —
St. Peter with a key & a book. A gilt Apostle spoon with ditto, ditto.

LEOPARD'S HEAD CROWNED (IN ROUND PUNCH)	NONE			1519	

— *One of a set from the Bernal Collection.* —
St. James the Greater with a Pilgrim's staff & a gourd. A gilt Apostle spoon with ditto, ditto.

LEOPARD'S HEAD CROWNED (IN ROUND PUNCH)	NONE			1519	

— *One of a set from the Bernal Collection.* —
St. Philip with a long staff & a book. A gilt Apostle spoon with ditto, ditto.

[L.C.]

PLATE IX

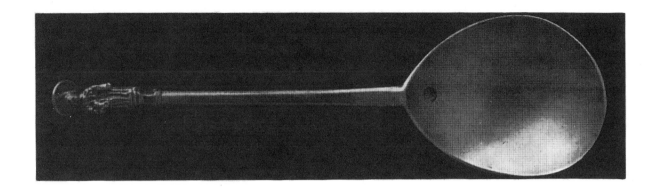

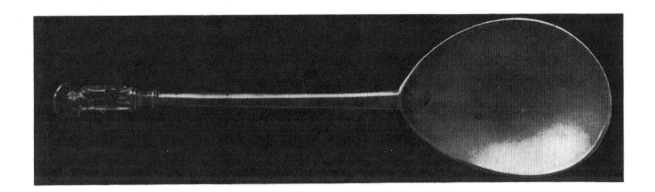

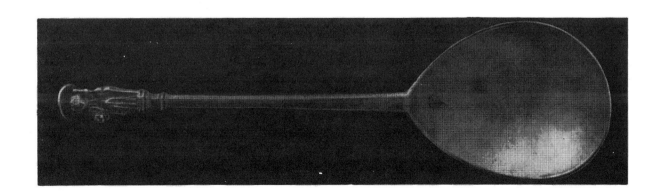

APOSTLE SPOONS

and bust of the Virgin Mary. No such set of fourteen, however, so far as can be ascertained, is in existence to-day.

A set of thirteen of these spoons was the favourite christening gift among the wealthy in Tudor and early Stuart times. In Shakespeare's *King Henry VIII*, Act V, Scene 3, Cranmer, who declares his unworthiness to act as godfather to "a fair young maid that yet wants baptism," is met with the rebuke from the King, "Come, come, My lord, you'd spare your spoons."

Persons of smaller means contented themselves with giving four spoons, representing the four Evangelists, and still poorer people with giving two, or, in many cases a single one, representing the Apostle after whom the child was to be named, or possibly the patron saint of the donor.

It is safe to say, in view of these gifts, that many an inquiring child in Tudor days had its first taste of religion with its milk, imbibed with the aid of an Apostle spoon.

The jealous preservation of these spoons by the parents of the recipient, and, later, by the recipient, now grown to man's or woman's estate, the social distinction which the possession of even one spoon conferred, and the meticulous bequest and mention in wills and inventories of these and other spoons, which were handed down from one generation to another, are responsible for the comparatively large number of excellent specimens that have survived. Spoons, moreover, had a high sentimental value, were readily concealed, and were of relatively light weight, and so, unlike heavier and less intimately personal silver articles, frequently escaped sale, seizure, and the melting-pot in time of financial distress, war and spoliation.

Apostles, however, were by no means the only spoons presented at christenings, and carefully preserved. Maidenheads, Lion Sejants, Seal-

APOSTLE SPOONS

tops, Slipped-in-the-stalks and others were often employed for the same purpose, as the pricking or engraving on many of them proves beyond any doubt.

The twelve Apostles generally represented may be distinguished generally by the following emblems :—

1. St. Peter holding one key, sometimes two, or a fish.
2. St. Andrew with a saltire cross, on which he suffered martyrdom.
3. St. James the Greater with a pilgrim's staff (as pioneer missionary), an escallop shell, or a hat and wallet.
4. St. John, with a cup, eagle, or palm branch.
5. St. Philip with a cross, long staff with a cross at the top, a basket of bread, several loaves, or a knotted cross.
6. St. Bartholomew, with a flaying knife, because he was flayed in his martyrdom.
7. St. Thomas, with a spear, arrow, girdle or builder's rule.
8. St. Matthew with a wallet, money-box, axe or T-square.
9. St. James the Less with a Fuller's bat, because he was killed by a blow on the head dealt him by Simeon the Fuller.
10. St. Jude, otherwise Thaddeus, with a carpenter's square, a cross, club, boat or inverted cross.
11. St. Simon Zelotes with a saw (in allusion to his martyrdom), a fish or an oar.
12. St. Matthias with a halberd, axe or lance.

St. Paul, who bears a sword, is sometimes substituted for one of the twelve.

All the twelve represented in the above list may be clearly identified on Plate XI.

The rarest spoon of the set, next to the Master, is probably St. Andrew. St. Peter, with a fish, is also a very scarce variety. The rare thirteenth spoon, the Master, is knopped with an image of Christ holding the orb and cross, the right hand upraised in blessing.

OLD SILVER SPOONS OF ENGLAND

The very early Apostle spoons may be distinguished by the fact that the nimbus or halo is set at the back of the Apostle's head, whereas, in later examples, it is inclined forward, and often pierced with holes for the light to penetrate the nimbus. The halo in some of the sixteenth, and almost every seventeenth century example, is formed by a circular disc affixed to the top of the head, and frequently bearing on the upper surface of the disc, emblematic of the descent of the Holy Ghost on the Apostle, a dove in low relief. These haloes have also served the purpose of protecting the little figures, which otherwise would frequently have been worn away.

Those who begin collecting Apostle spoons are sometimes puzzled by the discovery that an apparently perfectly genuine Apostle bears no emblem.

This is merely due to the fact that many of the emblems were wrought separately and affixed to the cast figure, the emblem frequently becoming broken off and lost during the centuries of the spoon's vicissitudes.

It is only of recent years that Apostle spoons have realised such high prices, although they have for long been objects of the collector's quest. The high watermark was reached at Christie's on July 16th, 1903, when a complete set of thirteen Henry VIII spoons, including the Master, was put up to auction.

The set was described as " the property of a gentleman in whose family they have descended as heirlooms for many generations past." Each spoon bore the London hall-mark, the date-letter for the year 1536–7, and the maker's mark, a Sheaf of Arrows.

The inside of the bowls bore the Sacred Monogram, in black-letter contemporary engraving on hatched ground, in a circle. Each spoon measured $7\frac{3}{4}$ inches long, the thirteen weighing 32 oz. 19 dwt.

APOSTLE SPOONS

Bidding started at £500, and at the sensational figure of £4,900 Mr. L. Hart, of Victoria Street, was declared the purchaser. This price works out at about £150 per oz. or £7 10s. per penny-weight.

The set is not only the earliest complete set of thirteen Apostles known to have survived, but its very existence was not recorded until a fortnight or so previous to the sale.

The fact that the Sacred Monogram, in the bowl of each spoon, had been executed before it was stamped with the Leopard's Head hall-mark, supports the theory that this particular set had been specially made for presentation to some Abbey.

An illustration of this wonderful set, designed to show particularly the images of the Master and various Apostles, appears on Plate XI by special permission of the present owner of the set.

These sets of thirteen Apostle spoons are of great rarity.

The Swettenham set of thirteen, all by one maker, and of the same date, 1617–18, was bought in at Christie's in 1897 for £650, and when put up again in 1901, realised £1,060. Another set of 1617–18 is owned by Mr. J. Pierpont Morgan. A set of twelve, of the year 1566–7, and a thirteenth, of the year 1515–16, believed to represent St. Paul, is in the possession of Corpus Christi College, Cambridge.

A set of twelve, dated 1637–8, realised £880 in 1910. Two spoons, by the same maker, one representing the Master, with the orb and cross, and the other the Apostle St. Philip, with a long staff and a basket of bread, both marked with the Lombardic " N," the date-letter for 1490–1, which had cost together £150, realised One Thousand Guineas for the pair in April, 1910.

Eleven Apostles of the year 1519–20, with the Fringed " S " for maker's mark, were bought by the Rev. Thomas Staniforth at the Bernal sale in 1855 for sixty-two guineas. The same eleven were sold by one of his descendants not very long ago for approximately £2,000.

A rather worn set of thirteen was sold at Christie's in 1901 for £1,060, and £1,200 would probably be the average price to-day of an early Stuart set. A spoon with a stem properly marked for a year in the reign of Henry VIII, but with an entirely new bowl, will sometimes fetch as much as £10 or more, merely for the stem and knop.

The sum of from £400 to £500 is frequently asked for a " mixed " set of twelve different Apostles and a Master of various dates and makers.

A set of eight Henry VIII Apostles, from the Marquis of Breadalbane's collection, bearing the London hall-mark, the date-letter for 1527-8, and the famous spiked letter S for maker's mark, realised 460 guineas at Christie's on May 12th, 1926. This was considered an unusually low price in view of the fine condition and early date of the set, but was partly explained by the facts that the sale took place during the General Strike, and that each spoon was punched with the name Breadalbane on the back of the stem.

The figures, which were surmounted by rayed nimbi, represented St. James the Less with a fuller's bat, St. Bartholomew with a flaying knife, St. Jude with a carpenter's square, St. James the Greater with a pilgrim's staff, St. Philip with a long staff, St. Matthias with an axe, St. Simon Zelotes with a long saw, and St. Andrew with a saltire cross.

Another Henry VIII apostle of 1531-2, bearing the same maker's mark, and knopped with the figure of St. Matthias, holding an axe, and with a rayed nimbus, realised fifty guineas at the same sale, and an Elizabethan Master spoon of 1584-5, the maker's mark, a mullet and a pellet, forty-five guineas.

APOSTLE SPOONS

The fringed or spiked letter S, that mysterious "touch" of the unknown silversmith, who flourished in the reigns of both Henry VII and Henry VIII, appears frequently on Apostle spoons, which find their way from time to time into the auction-room.

A Master spoon of 1530–1 with this mark, as described elsewhere, was sold for 100 guineas at the Charles James Toovey sale in February, 1926. A St. Andrew Apostle for 1492–3, and a St. John of 1495–6, both bearing this mark, were also sold at the beginning of this century for respectively £50 and £90.

A massive Apostle spoon, as large as a modern gravy-spoon, the property of the Worshipful Company of Plumbers, and engraved " The Guift of Richard Boult Feb : 17 : 1653," with S.V. as the maker's mark, was much commented on at the London Livery Companies' Exhibition at South Kensington in the summer of 1926.

Numerous illustrations of Master and Apostle spoons of various periods will be found on the Plates scattered throughout this book. Knops representing particular figures can be most readily identified by first consulting the index to the illustrations.

CHAPTER VII

Lion Sejants, Slipped-in-the-Stalks and Seal-Tops.

Lion Sejants, Slipped-in-the-stalks and Seal-tops, including the Pudsey and the Plague Spoons—Baluster-knops—The common characteristics of all old English Silver Spoons up to the end of the reign of Charles I—Fig- or pear- shaped bowls, hexagonal stems, stems and bowls hammered out of one piece—Pricking or pouncing of initials and dates.

LION SEJANTS

THE famous Lion Sejants (sejant—sitting; from the old French word *seiant*) are spoons topped with the gilt image of a small lion, which sits like a cat, with its fore-limbs stiff and upright, and frequently bears a shield on the front of its body.

One of the first references to these spoons is contained in the will of Sir Robert Le Strange, dated 1505, which mentions " a dosen Sponys wt lyons."

A Lion Sejant at South Kensington, however, from the H. D. Ellis collection, with the lion sitting sideways, and the mark a Closed Helmet, is ascribed to the fifteenth century (Illustration on Plate III). Another in the J. H. Walter collection, with the uncrowned Leopard's Head in a dotted circle, is assigned to about the year 1400. Three, all of

72

LION SEJANTS

1617-18 in the British Museum, have the initials I F with a Mullet and Pellets as the maker's mark.

Lion Sejants are known to have been popular spoons in Tudor times, and they continued to be produced well into the reign of James I, after which they were no longer made in London. Provincial specimens made in Exeter and other towns, however, are sometimes found as late as about 1640.

Lion Sejants and Maidenheads are among the rarest ancient English spoons to be met with in the auction-room to-day, and both are eagerly sought after by dealers and private collectors alike. Lion Sejants frequently realise upwards of thirty-five guineas apiece, even for provincial examples.

Other illustrations on Plates XV, XXIV, XXV and XXVI.

SLIPPED-IN-THE-STALKS

This spoon, of which the top appears to have been sliced off at an angle, just as a gardener slips a plant-stalk, frequently finds its way into the auction-room.

The earliest published reference to it appears in the will of Thomas Rotheram, Archbishop of York, dated 1498, which mentions a dozen silver spoons " slipped in lez Stalkes."

It is not without significance that this spoon, which, partly, no doubt, because of its simplicity, partly because of its lightness, was one of the most popular silver spoons in Tudor and early Stuart times, continuing to be made right up to the end of the reign of Charles I, and even a few years beyond, is nothing more than a reproduction, in one single piece of beautiful silver, of the primitive stick-and-shell spoon of savages and ancient man.

OLD SILVER SPOONS OF ENGLAND

PLATE X

MASTER, APOSTLE ST. THOMAS AND ST. JULIAN

REIGN OF HENRY VIII. SHOWING FRINGED "S" MARK

LEOPARD'S HEAD CROWNED (IN ROUND PUNCH)	NONE			1530	I . E ^G on the bowl.

The 'Saviour or 'Master' with an orb & cross, and hand raised in benediction, on his head a shaped nimbus pierced, (broken). Spoon with pear shaped bowl, hexagonal stem. — A fine example. —

LEOPARD'S HEAD CROWNED (IN ROUND PUNCH)	NONE			1537	

Apostle spoon, St Thomas with a spear, pear shaped bowl, hexagonal stem, on his head a nimbus with a star of eight rays.

[L.C.]

ST. JULIAN. LONDON, 1539–40. MAKER'S MARK, FRINGED "S" AS SHOWN ABOVE. [INNHOLDERS' COMPANY.]

PLATE X

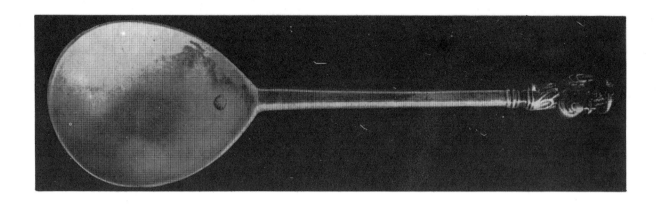

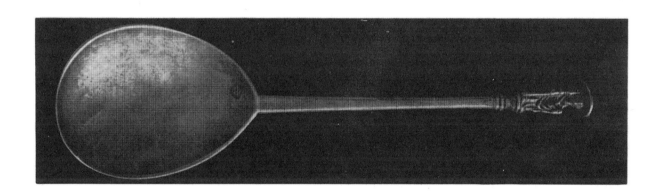

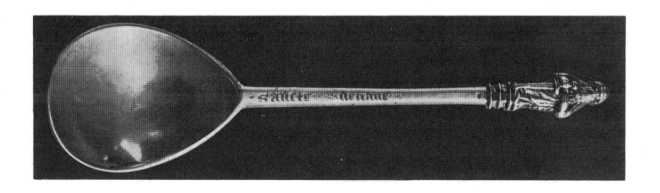

SLIPPED-IN-THE-STALKS

The close resemblance will be realised by a glance at one of the
" slip-top," or " slipped-end " spoons as they are otherwise called, in the
illustrations on Plates VII, VIII, XVIII and XX.

This spoon is sometimes incorrectly called the " Puritan " because
of its austere simplicity, and the reputed habit of Cromwell's adherents
of slicing off the figures of Apostle spoons as irreverent, the mutilated
spoons having much the appearance of Slipped-in-the-Stalks.

The real Puritan, or Commonwealth spoon, as will be seen later,
is a distinct variety. Small child's, or custard-spoon, slipped-ends,
about the size of a very large tea-spoon, are occasionally encountered,
and realise about £15 apiece.

The Slipped-in-the-Stalk ceased to be made after the first few years
of the Commonwealth, when the Puritan, with its flat stem and spade-
shaped bowl, superseded it. Slip-tops realise upwards of fifteen guineas
apiece for good London specimens of Charles I, sixteenth century
examples costing considerably more. A set of six, bearing the London
marks for 1622–3, and the maker's mark D enclosing C, was sold a few
years ago for £215.

SEAL-TOPS

The Baluster-and-Seal-headed spoon seems to have vied with the
Apostle spoon for popular favour in Tudor and early Stuart times.
These spoons continued to be made, with modifications in the forms
of the stems and the bowls, during the Commonwealth period, and,
during the first ten years of the Restoration, are said to have been the
favourite spoons of all.

Seal-headed spoons are found from the latter part of the fifteenth
century, right down to 1670, in the reign of Charles II, the silver-gilt

heads representing a number of beautiful and quaint varieties of form. They were great favourites during the reign of Queen Elizabeth.

The commonest form of seal-top has an acanthus leaf ornament beneath the lobes on which the seal rests.

A form of Seal-head frequently found in sixteenth century spoons has a baluster beneath the seal-head, but the long neck is absent.

The outline of the top on the earlier sixteenth century spoons, on the other hand, is frequently not circular but angular and octagonal, octagonal seals being particularly associated with the 1550 period. (Plate XII).

The once famous Pudsey spoon, now in the Mayer Museum, Liverpool, is an early example of the seal-top, and bears the London marks for 1525–6, with the maker's mark, a Heart. The upper surface of the seal is engraved with a five-petalled flower.

Tradition would have it that it was this spoon which was given by King Henry VI, who was deposed in 1461, and probably murdered in the Tower ten years later, to Sir Ralph Pudsey, of Bolton Hall, where that unfortunate monarch concealed himself for some weeks after the Battle of Hexham, the engraved flower being the rose, the badge of the King.

A careful examination has shown, however, that this could not have been the original spoon, as the dates do not agree. Not only is the Leopard's Head in the bowl found to be crowned, showing that it had been made after, and not before 1478, but the other marks show that the spoon was made in 1525–6.

Another famous Seal-top, bearing the London marks for 1653–4, and the property of Mr. T. W. Waller, is known as the " Plague Spoon." This title is due to the fact that the front of the shaft, or stele, of the spoon, bears an inscription reading as follows, " Rd in Ao 1665 when

OLD SILVER SPOONS OF ENGLAND

PLATE XI

VERY RARE SET OF THIRTEEN HENRY VIII APOSTLE SPOONS, INCLUDING THE MASTER, WHICH WAS SOLD FOR THE RECORD SUM OF £4,900 AT CHRISTIE'S, IN JULY, 1903. DATE, LONDON, 1536–7. MAKER'S MARK —A SHEAF OF ARROWS.

PLATE XI

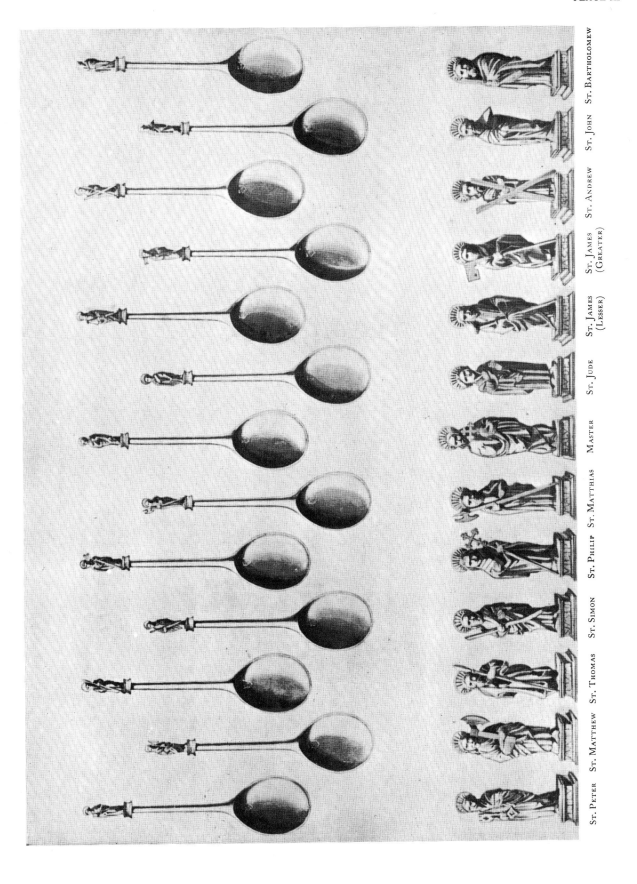

dyed at London of the plague 68596," the inscription continuing on the back of the shaft " . . . of all diseases 97306."

An unusual silver-gilt, late sixteenth century, Seal-top, from the Author's collection, now in the Victoria and Albert Museum, has the inside of the bowl and both sides of the stem richly engraved with characteristic ornamentation of the period. It is shown on Plate XII.

Seal-tops of unusually large size or heavy weight frequently realise very high prices.

An exceptionally heavy one, bearing the London marks for 1634–5, with the maker's mark B.V. above a Wicket Gate, sold at a public auction in 1903 for no less than £94, and another unusually heavy one of 1627–8, the maker's mark R.I. with a mullet beneath, for £90 at the same sale. Plates XII, XIII, XV, XVI, XVII, XVIII and XXIV.

BALUSTER-KNOPS

Some of the early Seal-tops have the end of the baluster above the seal. One of these is illustrated on Plate XIV.

A Queen Mary Baluster-knop, with the London marks of 1554–5, realised no less than £150 at a sale in June, 1920. This is probably a record figure for a Baluster-knop, which can be acquired, on occasion, for about one-quarter of that sum.

*   *   *   *   *

All the English silver spoons already mentioned, from the Acorn-knop to the Seal-top, up to the end of the reign of Charles I, have, with relatively few exceptions, a number of points in common.

These points may be summarised as follows :—All, with practically no exception whatever, have fig-shaped, or, as some people prefer to call them, pear-shaped bowls, with the narrower end or neck of the bowl, unlike the modern spoon, next to the stem, stele, or shaft.

An old English silver spoon, which has the broader end of the bowl towards the stem, may be safely assumed never to be earlier than the close of the reign of Charles I.

The stems are always roughly " six-squared," that is, six-sided or hexagonal, tapering slightly towards the top, although the sides may not be of equal width, and the wear of centuries may have given some of the stems the appearance of being almost four-sided, the upper and lower facets of the stem thus being wider than the other four facets.

Virtually the only exceptions to this rule are the stems of the fourteenth and fifteenth century spoons, which are generally either four-sided or diamond-section, or else appear to be almost rounded and bodkin-like, the bowls, however, retaining their pear-shaped form.

The sixteenth and seventeenth century spoons, with few exceptions, are of the modern dessert-spoon size, this size doing duty alike for table-spoons and dessert-spoons.

The tops or knops, particularly in the case of Apostles and Seal-tops, have generally retained their gilding, no matter if the whole spoon has been at one time gilt, and the gilt of the bowl and stem has worn partly or wholly away.

Stem and bowl are hammered out in one piece, the knop having been secured to the top of the stem by means of a soldered V joint.

The back of the bowl is strengthened by a short triangular stump or tail, a continuation of the stem, and one of the marks, in the case of London spoons the Leopard's Head, is always punched in the bowl.

The surfaces of the seals in Seal-tops, the shields in Lion Sejants, and the bowls or stems of these and other Tudor and Stuart spoons already mentioned, are frequently pricked or pounced, by a series of dots, or short lines, with one or more of the ancient owner's, or donor's, initials and possibly a date.

This pricking is an additional guarantee of the spoon's authenticity, such pricking being a lost art to-day. The date pricked, however, is necessarily no indication of the date of the spoon, the pricking being sometimes sixty years later than the date-letter punched on the stem, or even sixty years earlier, for that matter, the owner in the latter case possibly having wished to perpetuate the date of some past event or anniversary.

The pricked, or maybe engraved or scratched dates on spoons, were also frequently employed to record the year in which the spoon was presented or in which it changed hands.

CHAPTER VIII

LIST OF WONDERFUL SPOONS OF GOLD AND SILVER IN THE JEWEL BOOK OF KING HENRY VIII

LARGE numbers of valuable spoons were possessed by the English Kings and Queens, who set great store by them.

Some idea of the wonder and beauty of these treasures may be gathered from the Jewel Book of Henry VIII, in the library of the Society of Antiquaries of London.

Numerous priceless gold, silver or " white," and silver-gilt spoons, many of them enriched with enamels and precious stones, are carefully recorded in this famous Jewel Book.

Every one of these " spones of golde " and silver, alas, has apparently vanished. All were probably melted down by Charles I in the Civil War.

Cardinal Wolsey's magnificent collection of plate, including spoons, which was seized by Henry VIII, when he stripped the Prelate of his personal property, has also disappeared, without leaving a trace.

The Cardinal, like his King, employed his own goldsmith, one Robert Amadel, with five men to keep the plate constantly clean. The list of spoons in Henry's Jewel Book, it will be observed, includes not

OLD SILVER SPOONS OF ENGLAND

only Ball-knops, Lion Sejants, Maidenheads and Slipped-in-the-Stalks, but such examples, unknown to-day, as :—

Angel-knops	Four-bird-knops
Armorial-knops	Martlett-knops
Bud-knops	Pearl-knops
Columbynes	Rose-knops
Cross-knops	Ruby-knops
Deer's-foot-knops	Sickle-knops
Diamond-gem-knops	Square-knops
Falcon-knops	

The " Redd Roose " mentioned in connection with some of the knops is a favourite Tudor emblem.

The list of spoons makes fascinating reading. Every paragraph in the list begins with the word " Item " and mostly ends with the word " Poiz " or " Poz " (weighing).

It is scarcely necessary to mention that the figure " j " is equivalent to " i," H. viij meaning Henry VIII, ij oz.—2 ounces, and so on.

The list, extracted from the Jewel-Book, is as follows :—

INVENTORY OF THE KING'S JEWEL-HOUSE

20 Jany. 3 Edw. VI	SPONES OF GOLDE	Poiz (weighing)
One Spone of golde graven with an H. and a Roose		one ounce qurt' di
A Spone of gold wt a rubie at the end . . .		ij oz. di quart
A Spone of gold with a wrythen stele having a Scripture abowte it the kinges armes crowned in the topp gyven by the lorde Marques of Excetor uppon Neweyeres day anno xxvo H. viij . .		ij oz. iij qut' di
A Spone of gold with a playne knopp vj squared withowte any graving therein gyven by the Lorde Dawbeney anno xxvijmo nuper R.H. viij		ij oz. skant

82

SPOONS OF KING HENRY VIII

SPONES OF GOLDE—(*continued*)
Poiz
(weighing)

A Spone of gold with a playne square stele and a di
knopp with a roose at the end half white and half
redd receaved of the kinges grace that ded is in
lewe of a spone receaved by his grace owte of his
pantrye . . . . ij ounces

A Spone of gold with a knopp six squared and the
stele vj squared gyven by the Ladie Marques
Dorsett on New yeres daye anno xxixo nuper H.
viij . . . . ij oz. di qurt'

A small Spone of gold having a stele six squared and
verey small chased the knopp being six squared
gyven by therle of Bridgewater on Newe-yeres daye
Anno xxxo nuper H. viij . . . . . one oz. di

One Spone of gold the stele vj squared the knopp at
theend vj squared having thereuppon enameled
a roose white and redd gyven by the lorde Stafford
the saide daye and yere . . . . . one oz. iij qurt' di

A Spone of gold with a wrethen stele and a double
roose white and redd at theend . . . . ij oz.

A Spone of gold with a knopp six squared therein the
kinges armes graven gyven by the lorde Dawbeney
anno xxviiimo nuper H. viij . . . . ij oz. quart'

One Spone of gold with a iiij square stele twooe squares
thereof graven or chased with a three squared
knopp in the myddes and on a plate at theende
the kinges armes graven and enameled . . iij oz di quart'

One Spone of gold with a flatt stele twoo partes thereof
enameled blacke likewise parte of the knopp
having a plate therein the kinges armes graven
and enameled thereuppon . . . . . iiij oz di qurt'

A Spone of gold with a stele chased and a rounde
knopp having a dyamounte sett in the ende . iij oz. d qurt'

A Spone of gold the stele turned rounde with a rounde
knopp and a redd roose and a white at the end
weying . . . . iiij oz.

OLD SILVER SPOONS OF ENGLAND

PLATE XII

BEAUTIFUL EXAMPLES IN THE NATIONAL COLLECTION

(1) OCTAGONAL SEAL-TOP OF THE TIME OF HENRY VIII. LONDON, 1543–4. MAKER'S MARK, A FRINGED "S."

(2) MAIDENHEAD. DATE, ABOUT 1550?

(3) APOSTLE ST. JOHN, WITH AN EAGLE. LONDON, 1610–11.

(4) MAIDENHEAD. ABOUT 1530.

(5) ENGRAVED SILVER-GILT SEAL-TOP. FROM THE AUTHOR'S COLLECTION. DATE ABOUT 1590. NO MARKS.

[V. AND A. M.]

PLATE XII

1   2   3   4   5

SPOONS OF KING HENRY VIII

SPONES OF GOLDE—(*continued*)
Poiz
(weighing)

One other Spone of gold the stele six squared the
knopp allso six squared with a Lion graven uppon
the end . . . . ij oz.

Twoo spones of gold the haftes of theym being writhen
one of theym hathe the kinges armes at thone
ende and thother a roose, poiz togethers . . iiij oz. iij qrt' and
ijsvjdwt

One Spone of gold wrought uppon the stele with
leaves and a redd flower uppon the topp . . iij ounces
Receaved of Sr John Gate knight parcell of the
plate carried in the removing cofers for bankettes
as before

A Spone of gold with a flatt stele the kinges armes
enameled uppon the knopp . . . . iiij oz.

A Spone of gold the handle rounde embossed with
leaves like chessemen and a rounde knopp . . iiij oz. iij qrters di.

A Spone of gold having a roose in the knopp enameled
white and redd . . . . . . ij oz. quart' di
Receaved of Willm Sayntbarbe one of the gromes
of the kinges Mates pryvey Chambr ixo July
Re E. vjti pimo parcell of the dyett plate

A Spone of Gold the handle being wrythen the kinges
armes enameled at the ende . . . . ij oz. di

A Spone of golde foure squared the kinges armes
enameled at the end . . . . . ij oz. di quart'
Receaved at Hampton Courte of the saide Sr
Thomas Cawarden as before

Twoo spones of gold with twoo Lions holding twoo
Scutchions with the kinges armes enameled at
thendes . . . . viij oz.

One Straynera of gold with a roose at thende . . iij cz.
Receaved the xjth of July 1547 pcell of the night
plate founde in a square house in the long gallorie
at Westminster

85

OLD SILVER SPOONS OF ENGLAND

A little Spone of golde with a perle at thende .   .   j qurter di of an ounce
    Receaved at Hampton Courte owte of the kinges
    owne Juelhous as before

viij Spones of golde of sondrie sortes whereof one
    hathe a knopp of perle   .   .   .   .   xxij oz. di
    Receaved at Hampton Courte late in the Custodie
    of David Vincent. A spone of golde   .   iij oz.
    Receaved at Windesor as before:

One Spone of gold the stele being wrought with leaves
    and a Scripture enameled having a white Martlett
    in the topp   .   .   .   .   .   .   ij oz. iij qurters

One Spone of gold with a wrethe abowte the stele and
    a roose in the topp   .   .   .   .   ij oz. quart
    Receaved at Otelandes of the said Sr Thomas
    Cawarden Knight

Twoo spones of gold thone having a roose at thend
    and thother a ffawcon crowned   .   .   iiij oz. di qurt'
    Receaved owte of the said Secrete Juelhous in
    tholde gallorie as Westmr as before

xv Spones of cristall garnished with gold thone of
    theym lacking the boll poiz togethers   .   .   xvj oz. di di qurt

One Spone of gold the stele enameled and a white
    Lyon at thende thereof   .   .   .   .   j oz. iij qrters

One Spone of gold the stele wrought wt an Aungell
    bearing a libbardes hedd uppon a Scutchion   .   ij oz. di di qurter

A Spone of golde the stele enameled blacke with the
    kinges armes enameled at thende thereof   .   .   iiij oz. quart'

One spone of golde the stele enameled blacke with a
    roose at thende thereof   .   .   .   .   ij oz. quarter

One Spone of golde with the kinges armes enameled
    at thend .   .   .   .   ij oz. quart' di

One Spone of gold having a Lion holding a ring in his
    clawe   .   .   .   .   one oz. di di quart'

One Spone of gold the stele having a ragged thing
    abowte it and a white and a redd roose at thend
    thereof   .   .   .   .   .   .   one oz. di

OLD SILVER SPOONS OF ENGLAND

PLATE XIII

HEXAGONAL-KNOP AND SEAL-TOPS

EARLY ELIZABETHAN

HEXAGONAL-KNOP. LONDON, 1565–6. MAKER'S MARK, R.K., MULLET BELOW. FORMERLY BELONGING TO WHITTINGTON COLLEGE. [MERCERS' COMPANY]

HALL	STANDARD	MAKER	LETTER	DATE	INITIALS &c
LEOPARD'S HEAD CROWNED	LION PASSANT			1558	T·E on the button.

Spoon, with pear shaped bowl, hexagonal stem, baluster & seal top

LEOPARD'S HEAD CROWNED	LION PASSANT			1563	A·S on the button.

Spoon, gilt, pear shaped bowl, hexagonal stem, baluster & seal top.
— Of stout make. —

[L.C.]

PLATE XIII

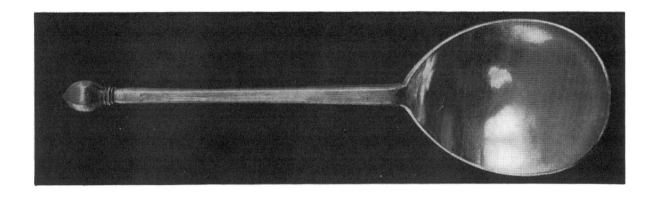

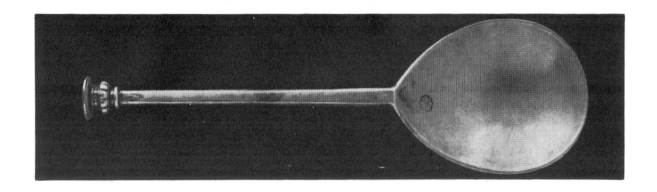

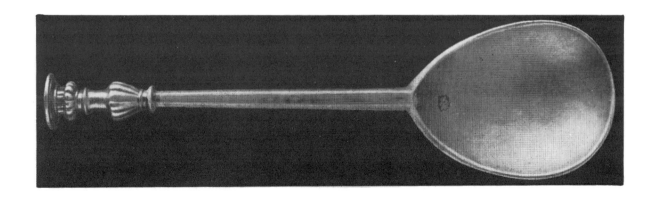

| 20 Jany. | SPONES OF GOLDE—*(continued)* | Poiz |
| 3 Edw. VI | | (weighing) |

One Spone of gold the stele partly enameled blacke
    and a rounde knopp . . . . .   one oz. quart' di

Twoo Spones of gold with H. and J. at thende of theym   iij oz. di di quart

A Spone of gold with H.A. crowned at thende thereof   ij ounces

A Spone of gold with armes of foure birdes and other
    things in yt at thende thereof . . . .   ij ounce

A Spone of gold with a deeres foote at thende of the
    stele . . . .   ij ounces

One Spone of gold with a playne knopp . . .   ij oz. iij qurt' di

SPONES

    Receaved of the said Remayne

Fourtene Spones well gilt slipped at thendes . .   xxvj ounces di

xvij gilt. Spones wt half knoppes and Staffordes
    knottes at thendes . . . . . .   xxxij ounces iij quarters

Five Spones gilt wt Rooses in the knoppes . .   ix oz. iij q'trs di

Five Spones gilt wt Buddes of the knoppes . .   vij ounces

xj Spones gilt . . . .   xxij oz.

vj Spones wt knoppes vj squared at thendes marked
    wt a Crossbow and Esses bought of Cornelis .   xj ounces qurter

Two gilt Spones wt the lre R the knoppes like Rooses
    and rounde bought of John Freeman goldsmithe
    thone spone to make up vj Spones with the vth
    entered in this Booke before and there weing ix oz.
    iij qutre di and thother spone to make upp xij
    Spones wt the xjth entres in this Boke before
    weing xxij oz. thes two Spones poiz . . .   iij ounces iij qurters di

Five gilt Spones wt thappostells at their endes . .   x ounces quarter

xij silver Spones wt gilt Columbynes at the endes .   xxiij ounces di

Eight Spones white with thappostells at the endes gilt   xiiij oz.

Tenne other Spones white slipped at thendes weing
    together . . . .   xv ounces iij quarters

Twelve Spones white slipped at thendes gilt . .   xxviij ounces

Twelve Spones white wt diamoundes knoppes weing
    together . . . .   xj ounces iij quarters

SPOONS OF KING HENRY VIII

SPONES—(*continued*)

Poiz
(weighing)

vj White Spones slipped at their endes . . . (no weight given)

Foure white Spones wt thes lres graven at thendes
H and R weing together . . . . . viij oz. di

lxvj Spones gilt of divers sortes and sundrey makings
together . . . . Cxxxij ounces iij
quarters

Twelve gilt Sponez wt vj squared knoppes and squared
steeles all striken wt the lre .E . . . xxiij oz. quarter

Twelve gilt Spones wt vj squared knoppes and squared
steeles all striken wt the lre .C . . . xxiij oz. quarter

Twelve gilt Spones wt vj squared knoppes at theendes
and all striken wt a small B. . . . . xxx oz. di

ix gilt Spones wt gilt Apostelles at the endes one being
of another sorte striken with an H and eight
striken wt an A . . . . . . xix oz. di

ix gilt spones wt vj squared knoppes at the endes and
roses graven theruppon striken with H and one
with a harte . . . . xix oz.

Foure gilt spones of severall sortes thone with Christ
at thende another wt one of the Apostelles at
thende the thirde wt an Angell at thende and the
fourth wt a Crowne at thende weing together . x oz. di quarter

Five Spones sumtyme gilt : gilt (sic) three theref wt
womens heddes and faces and thother two with
Lyons . . . . vj ounces

Tenne spones parcell gilt wt thappostelles at thendes xv ounces iij quarters

Foure Spones gilt thone wt a Columbyne at thende
striken wth a D tother two with squared knoppes
striken with a T or R ; the fourthe being almost
white, slipped at thende . . . . . vij ounces quarter

xxiiij Spones of Silver gilt wherof xij hathe Sicles at
ther endes . . . . xlix oz.

One Suckett Spone wt a forke Joyned together
of silver gilte . . . . iij oz.

One Spone of Silver gilt. thandle with a Roose . ij ounces

One Spone wt a suckett forke uppon one stele gilt iij ounces

89

SPONES—(*continued*)

	Poiz (weighing)
ix Spones of silver and gilt with the Lorde Crumwelles armes at their endes	xxiiij oz. quarter
Foure spones of white bone the steelez of Imagies of white bone in Tabernacles of silver and gilt the rest of the steelez of silver and gilt . . .	vij ounces di quarter
Eight Spones of mother of peerle thaftez of silver and gilt	vij ounces di
One spone of Christall garneshed and thaftes of silver and gilt	one oz.
One Spone of Cerpentyne the steele and part thereof of silver and gilt wt a Crosse at thende and wordez graven	one oz. quarter
One spone of silver and gilt wt thafte of glasse at thende thereof a Columbyne of silver gilt . . .	one ounce iij quarters di
Three sponez of pied bone garneshed withe silver gilt	ij oz. quarter
Twelve Sponez of mother or peerle the steeles of silver and gilt and twelve forkes of silver and gilt .	xvij ounces quarter
Two sponez of cristall the steelez of silver and gilt of sundry sortes weing together	ij ounces
vj Sponez of welke shelles every of them garneshed slightlie wt silver	(no weight given)
One spone wt suckett forke at thende of silver and gilt	one oz. iij qurter
v Spones of Cristall garnysshed wt golde enameled	

One of the several puzzling items in the foregoing list is the spoon of which the stele or stem is described as " having a ragged thing abowte it."

The "spone wt suckett forke at thende," was no doubt one of those used in Tudor times for the eating of sweetmeats. The British Museum possesses a small specimen of this variety.

CHAPTER IX

The Coming of the Great Change in the Form of Ancient Spoons

Change in the relative proportions of the bowl—Stems no longer six-sided—The Puritan or Stump-Top—Melting down of spoons for munition and siege money in the Civil War—Siege-piece that was a spoon-bowl, the Leopard's Head still intact—Buried spoons—Example of spoons' influence in the politics of nations—Butler's *Hudibras*.

Appearance of the Lobed-End, variously called the Trifid, Trefoil, Split-End, Notched-Top or *Pied de Biche*, with its rat-tailed and spade-shaped bowl, the narrower portion of the bowl now, for the first time, at the base or lip.

Lobed-ends the most inexpensive form of early ancient spoon now available— Shield-tops or Waved-Ends with "cats' heads and rats' tails"—End of the centuries of picturesque spoon-tops—Arrival of the "Hanoverian" pattern.

I

THE latter part of the reign of Charles I saw the beginning of the great change in the form and appearance of old silver spoons. The Maidenheads and Lion Sejants had ceased to be made with the end of the reign of James I, except in the provinces, leaving only the Apostle, Seal-top and Slipped-in-the-Stalk; but a far greater change impended. Silver spoons, for more than two centuries, it may be repeated, had shared two common characteristics. The first was a fig- or pear-shaped bowl, with the "neck," or considerably narrower portion of the bowl, towards the handle or stem.

The second characteristic was a six-sided or hexagonal stem, the fourteenth and fifteenth century spoons possibly excepted, as already noted.

OLD SILVER SPOONS OF ENGLAND

The bowl, towards the end of the reign of the ill-fated Charles Stuart, however, underwent a gradual, but marked, transformation.

The handle of the Apostle, Seal-top or Slipped-end became at this period flatter to the sight and touch, the upper and lower facets growing wider, and the other four facets so narrow as almost to disappear. Disappear they did for all time in the flat-stemmed spoons of Cromwell's time, the famous Puritan spoons. The bowl, also, became first narrower in proportion at the lower end, then wider at the part nearest the stem, assuming, at the end of Charles I's reign, almost a true ellipse, the change in the bowl continuing until, by the middle of the Commonwealth, the bowl became definitely wider at the top and narrower at the base, never to return to its old form. The egg-shaped bowl persists to this day. The change is shown at a glance in the first three spoons illustrated together on Plate XX.

PURITANS OR STUMP-TOPS

Opinion is divided as to the real origin of the famous Puritan Stump-top, or Square-end, spoon, with its spade-shaped bowl. The Slipped-end is sometimes miscalled the Puritan, because the Puritan soldiers opposed to Charles were said to have considered Apostle spoons irreverent, and to have formed the habit of summarily slicing off with their swords the images of the Apostles from all Apostle spoons they encountered.

The Puritan spoon, with its spade-shaped bowl, and its long, flat stem, is certainly a marvellously simple spoon of a beautiful austerity.

The stem is two-sided and flat as a strip of tooth- or shaving-cream, having frequently, although by no means invariably, two notches cut at the extreme top of the stem. The Puritan stem seems to have been

92

evolved simply by hammering thinner the stem of the Slipped-in-the-Stalk.

The entire spoon, like the Slipped-in-the-Stalk which preceded it, is made out of a single piece of silver. (Illustrations on Plates XIX and XX.)

The Puritan silver spoon came in with the end of the reign of Charles I, one of the earliest Carolean specimens known bearing the date-letter of the year 1640–1, and one of the earliest Commonwealth examples, of the year 1651–2.

Little new silver plate of any kind was made during this troublous period, and Commonwealth spoons, like other silver of the period, are comparatively scarce, and eagerly sought after. Sets of small custard spoons, a little larger than the biggest of modern tea-spoons, now made their appearance, as did the long-stemmed "Hash" spoons.

Small size Puritan spoons sometimes find their way into the auction-rooms, where they realise anywhere from £15 apiece, and £100 for a set of six.

Silver spoons, like other priceless silver that can never be replaced, were, at this time, being melted down by King and Parliament for the sinews of the Civil War.

How many hundredweights of precious silver spoons of Charles I's time, and of preceding reigns, went into the melting-pot to make money with which to pay the troops and provide munitions will never be known. Hosts of Acorn-knops, Diamond-points, Maidenheads, Wrythen-knops, Apostles, Seal-tops, Slipped-ends, and Lion Sejants, particularly Carolean Apostles, Slipped-ends and Seal-heads, must have shared the same fate, although spoons, because of their comparative light weight, their intimate sentimental value, and the facility with which they might be concealed, were probably the last silver articles to be melted down.

OLD SILVER SPOONS OF ENGLAND

PLATE XIV

BALUSTER-TOP, MAIDENHEAD AND APOSTLE: ST. SIMON

EARLY ELIZABETHAN

HALL	STANDARD	MAKER	LETTER	DATE	INITIALS &c
LEOPARD'S HEAD CROWNED	LION PASSANT		t	1576	1659 on the button

Seal top spoon, pear shaped bowl, hexagonal stem with baluster top projecting through the button.

HALL	STANDARD	MAKER	LETTER	DATE	INITIALS &c
LEOPARD'S HEAD CROWNED	LION PASSANT		A	1578	on back of bowl in faint outline. AD 1578

Spoon with gilt knob of a maiden's head and bust, hair flowing down the back, pear shaped bowl, hexagonal stem.

HALL	STANDARD	MAKER	LETTER	DATE	INITIALS &c
LEOPARD'S HEAD CROWNED	LION PASSANT		A	1578	On the front of stem is inscribed :- NATA·ANO·DNI·1578·OCTOB·10· A·H INTER·HOR·12·ET·PRI·IN·AVRORA SUSCEPTORE·GVAL·MOYE

Gilt Apostle spoon; St Simon with a saw, on his head a nimbus with plain convex top, hexagonal stem, pear shaped bowl, stoutly made.
—— A very fine example. ——

[L.C.]

PLATE XIV

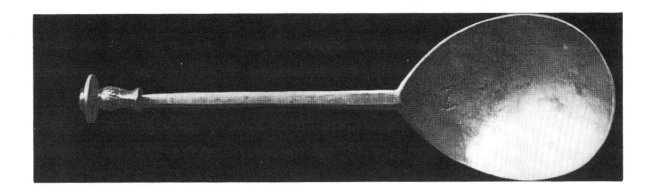

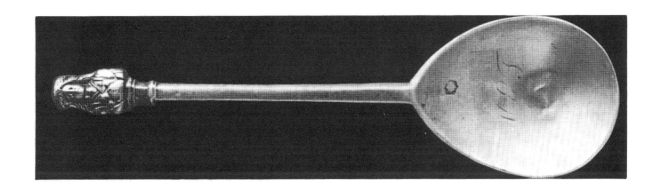

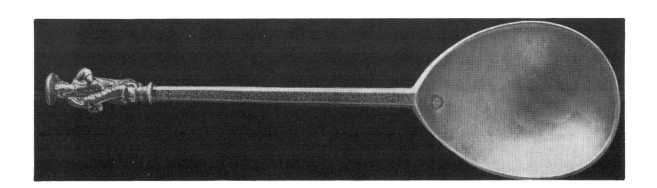

CHANGE IN FORM OF ANCIENT SPOONS

Melted down, however, they were; for not once, but many times, have silver spoons made their influence felt in the politics of nations.

Enormous masses of plate, including silver spoons, were heaped up in the Guildhall by the citizens of London in support of the cause of the Parliament against Charles I, and other towns and cities followed suit. A single illustration from the provinces may be mentioned :—

The list of donors to the Parliamentary cause, and their gifts. named in *The History of Antiquities of Great Yarmouth*, published in Norwich in 1772, included the following :—

" Thomas Goose, seven pieces of plate and two spoons."

" Robert Wakeman . . . nine spoons in coarse silver weighing 14 oz. at 4s. 6d. per oz."

" William Burton 59 oz. plate, one spoon, best, and four coarse spoons . . . and a bodkin."

" George England 91 oz. and seven silver spoons."

" Robert Huntington, 158 oz. and one spoon.

" William Bridge fourteen spoons."

" John Thompson, two cups and a spoon."

Butler, champion of monarchy, thus ridicules them in *Hudibras*— Canto II :—

> "A thimble, bodkin and a spoon
> Did start up living men as soon
> As in the furnace they were thrown."

Quantities of plate were also melted down for Charles I's siege-money, and one of his famous Siege-piece coins, which recently came to light, showed that it had been fashioned by merely shaping an old spoon-bowl, which had actually retained its Leopard's Head.

Numbers of spoons made about the time of the Civil War, however, were buried by their owners, who never returned to claim them. Many

95

examples have been dug up from time to time in London and the provinces, the corrosion of the marks and the pitting of the bowls indicating their tragic history.

Both the Puritan and the Seal-top—and also a certain number of Apostles—continued to be made for perhaps ten years after the Restoration.

One of the new forms of late Commonwealth and early Restoration Puritan Square-end or Stump-top was a sort of exaggerated Puritan, with the flat stem widening considerably as it reaches the top. It is shown in the centre of Plate XX.

The Puritan, then, was made approximately from 1640 to about the year 1668–9, when a spoon, like, yet unlike, took its place.

LOBED-ENDS, VARIOUSLY CALLED TRIFIDS, TREFOILS, SPLIT-ENDS OR PIEDS-DE-BICHE

The new spoon was the Lobed-end, Trefoil, Split-end, Trifid or Notched-end, as it is variously described, a variety which is frequently miscalled the *Pied-de-Biche*, because of the supposed resemblance of the top of the handle to a hind's foot.

The Lobed-end is said to have been introduced from France, but appears, on the other hand, to be a logical development of the Puritan, the two slight nicks or notches frequently found cut at the top of the Puritan spoon being deepened in the case of the Trifid, so that it has three distinct lobes turned slightly upwards. The early Lobed-end, with its thin, flat stem and either spade-shaped or oval bowl, appears otherwise, when viewed from the front, closely to resemble the Puritan although, in the majority of Trifids, the Leopard's Head or other

96

CHANGE IN FORM OF ANCIENT SPOONS

Town-Mark is no longer punched in the bowl, but on the back of the stem with the other marks.

A closer inspection of the back of the stem, however, reveals one very marked difference. This is the appearance of a long clearly-defined tongue or rat-tail, more than half-way down at the back of the bowl, for the first time in the history of old English silver spoons, the old form of " tail," however, which is actually the finishing off of the lower part of the stem in a short angle, frequently continuing to be made in the provinces well into the reign of James II.

The Lobed-end is one of the early ancient spoons, whose relatively small cost brings it within the reach of collectors of modest means, and some collectors confine their acquisitions to this one variety. Lobed-ends, which first appeared early in the reign of Charles II, retained their popularity during the reigns of James II, William and Mary, and William III, and continued well into the reign of George I, although most of them had ceased to be made a few years after Anne ascended the throne.

They show numerous variations of the characteristic lobed-top and of the rat-tail. The backs of many of the bowls and the upper portions of the fronts of the stems, particularly those of Charles II, are beautifully decorated with foliage in relief, and these varieties are the particular quest of collectors, commanding considerably higher prices than the undecorated examples.

Lobed-ends made in the Netherlands about the late seventeenth and early eighteenth centuries closely resemble the English varieties.

An interesting Flemish " In Memoriam " Lobed-end, from the Author's collection, in the Victoria and Albert Museum, is virtually indistinguishable from an English Lobed-end of the time of William

97

and Mary, apart from the marks. It bears engraved on the back of the bowl, in addition to the name of a man and the precise date of his death in the year 1714, an inscription which, translated, reads as follows :

"O Men, as you are, so I was.
And as I am, so you will become."

A plain Lobed-end made in the provinces, with marks known as "unascribed," may be acquired for as little as £2 or £3, whereas a Charles II London-made "Decorated Back," or one with a rare provincial mark, brings often as much as £10 or £15 or £100 for a set of six, by the same maker, and all bearing the same date-letter.

Handsomely engraved bowls and stems were characteristic of the Lobed-ends of William and Mary. Illustrations on Plates XX, XXI, XXII, XXIII and XXVI.

SHIELD-TOPS OR WAVED ENDS

These, which are sometimes described as Cat-head, Rat-tail spoons, the shield-top vaguely suggesting the silhouette of the head of a cat, came in with the reign of James II. They represent, in form, Lobed-ends from which both outer lobes have disappeared. The rat-tails are invariably present.

An unusually early Shield-top of James II, bearing the date-letter for 1685–6, was auctioned off at the Breadalbane sale in May, 1926.

The majority of the Shield-tops encountered by collectors date from the time of William III. They disappeared, generally, with the Lobed-ends early in the reign of Queen Anne. Transitional Shield-tops have the one remaining lobe hammered back or curled over. Illustrations on Plate XXVII.

OLD SILVER SPOONS OF ENGLAND

PLATE XV

APOSTLE, ST. JOHN, SEAL-TOP AND LION SEJANT

LATE ELIZABETHAN

HALL	STANDARD	MAKER	LETTER	DATE	INITIALS &c
LEOPARD'S HEAD CROWNED	LION PASSANT	(maker's mark)	M	1589	

Apostle spoon with gilt statuette of St. John holding the cup of sorrow and right hand raised in benediction, hexagonal stem, pear shaped bowl, pierced nimbus.—Of stout make and in good preservation.—

HALL	STANDARD	MAKER	LETTER	DATE	INITIALS &c
LEOPARD'S HEAD CROWNED	LION PASSANT	(maker's mark)	M	1589	(monogram) on the button

Seal top spoon with short hexagonal stem, pear shaped bowl.

HALL	STANDARD	MAKER	LETTER	DATE	INITIALS &c
LEOPARD'S HEAD CROWNED	LION PASSANT	(maker's mark)	H	1585	G$^{C}_{E}$ also E·L on the back of bowl.

Spoon, pear shaped bowl, hexagonal stem with a gilt lion sejant on the end.

[L.C.]

PLATE XV

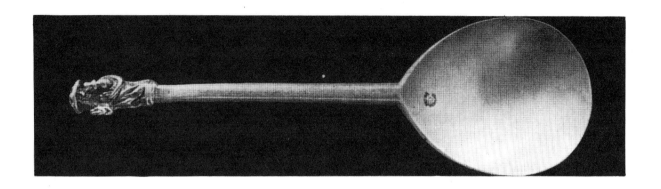

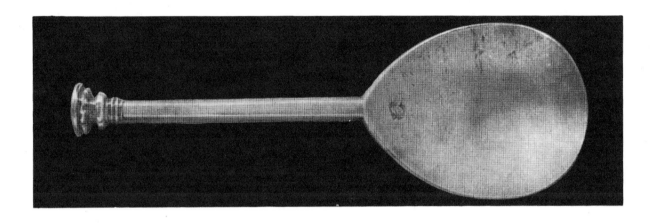

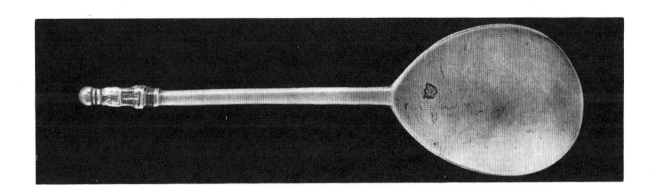

OLD SILVER SPOONS OF ENGLAND

THE "HANOVERIAN" RAT-TAILS

Most of the spoons of the time of Queen Anne which find their way into the sale's room to-day are neither Lobed-ends nor Shield-tops, although they retain their Rat-tails.

The flatness of the entire stem, which has persisted since Cromwellian times, has disappeared, and, although the now-thickened end turns still upward towards the face of the spoon, a sharp rib runs from the top to half-way down the front of the stem. This type is seen at a glance on Plate XXVII.

This entirely new form of Rat-tailed spoon was introduced about 1705, and continued to be made for about twenty-five years. It is frequently miscalled the Hanoverian pattern spoon because its introduction coincided roughly with the accession of the House of Hanover in the person of George I.

The centuries-old reign of the " early " old English spoons, with their picturesque handles and knops, was now at an end.

CHAPTER X

THE MARKS ON OLD LONDON SPOONS

The Leopard's Head, Maker's Mark and Date Letter—Introduction of the Lion
Passant—The Britannia Figure and Lion's Head Erased—The Sovereign's
Head—Significance of Leopard's Head which is punched in the bowl or
spoon-self of Pre-Tudor, Tudor, Early Stuart and Commonwealth spoons
—Leopard's Head uncrowned often sign of very early London spoons—
Birds, animals and other symbols used as early Makers' Marks—The Key,
Heart, Eagle Displayed, Sun, Sheaf of Arrows, Bird's Claw and Crescent—
Date-letters—Books on Silver-marks.

I

GROWING evidence tends to establish that more than ninety
per cent. of all the gold and silver plate wrought in the
British Isles up to 1770 bore the London hall-mark,
and withstood the tests imposed by the Worshipful Company of
Goldsmiths.

The punched marks on old silver spoons have certainly an
important bearing for the collector on the authenticity, rarity and value
of the piece, the period or year in which it was made, its town of origin
or assay, and, in many instances, the actual identity and business
address of its maker, centuries, it may be, ago.

It was enacted by Statute, as far back as 1300, that a
distinguishing mark or marks should be stamped on all English-made

OLD SILVER SPOONS OF ENGLAND

PLATE XVI

MASTER SPOON AND SEAL-TOPS

LATE JAMES I AND LATE CHARLES I

HALL	STANDARD	MAKER	LETTER	DATE	INITIALS &c
LEOPARD'S HEAD CROWNED	LION PASSANT	RC	V	1617	

Seal top spoon, hexagonal stem, pear shaped bowl. Small and slender make.

HALL	STANDARD	MAKER	LETTER	DATE	INITIALS &c
LEOPARD'S HEAD CROWNED	LION PASSANT	D	V	1617	Married Sep 13th 1819 underneath crest outside bowl. & John William Born inside bowl

Apostle spoon. The Saviour with the orb and cross, the right hand raised in benediction, a dove on the nimbus, hexagonal stem, pear shaped bowl. — Stout make – A fine example. —

HALL	STANDARD	MAKER	LETTER	DATE	INITIALS &c
LEOPARD'S HEAD CROWNED	LION PASSANT	I·I		1642	I $\frac{N}{M}$ on back of bowl.

Seal top spoon, hexagonal stem, baluster knob, pear shaped bowl.

[D. C.]

PLATE XVI

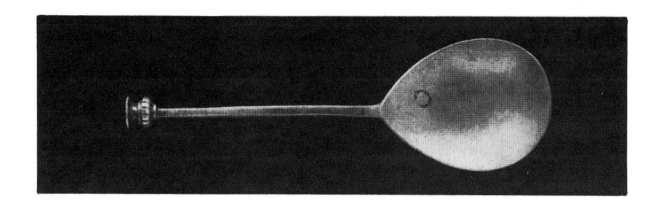

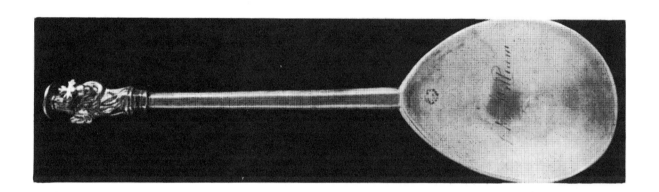

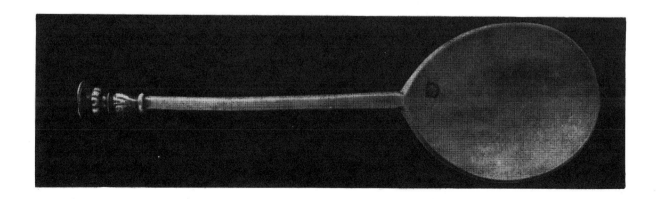

MARKS ON OLD LONDON SPOONS

silver, including spoons, and even at that early date the mark was described "as of ancient use." Such marks were probably struck as early as the twelfth century. This law, however, for very many years, was frequently ignored or disobeyed.

Spoons of the fourteenth, fifteenth, sixteenth, and even seventeenth centuries may, therefore, be perfectly genuine if bearing only the maker's mark, or possibly no marks at all. The eye of an expert can readily establish their authenticity, and in many instances fix their date within a margin of only a few years. Numbers of priceless early English spoons in the possession of museums and famous collectors bear incomplete marks or none at all. The marks were ordained originally solely for the purpose of preventing fraud.

Old London silver spoons from 1478, in the reign of Edward IV, up to the year 1543, in the reign of Henry VIII, should bear the three following marks, the first shown in the spoon-bowl below :—

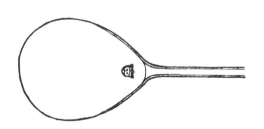

(a) The Leopard's Head, stamped in the bowl.

(b) Maker's mark on back of stem, generally at meeting of stem and handle.

(c) Date-letter, that is a letter of the alphabet which was changed annually, also on back of stem.

From 1544 to the end of March, 1697, they should bear four as follows :—

(a) Leopard's Head stamped in the bowl up to about 1665 and afterwards on back of stem.

(b) Maker's mark on back of stem.

(c) Date-letter on back of stem.

(d) Lion Passant on back of stem.

THE LION  PASSANT

103

OLD SILVER SPOONS OF ENGLAND

From the end of March, 1697, to 1718–19, the following four were stamped, all on the back of the stem :—

BRITANNIA FIGURE  LION'S HEAD ERASED

(a) Figure of Britannia instead of Leopard's Head.
(b) Maker's Mark.
(c) Date-letter.
(d) Lion's Head Erased.

From 1719–20 to 1783–4 these four on the back of the handle :

(a) Leopard's Head.
(b) Maker's Mark.
(c) Date-Letter.
(d) Lion Passant.

From 1784–5 to 1785–6 the following marks on the back of the stem—five marks now :—

(a) Leopard's Head.
(b) Maker's Mark.
(c) Date-Letter.
(d) Lion Passant.
(e) King's Head, in profile turned to the left.

From 1786–7 to 1836–7. The same five marks, except that the King's Head is turned in profile to the right.

From 1837–8 to 1895–6. The same five, except that the profile of the sovereign, now a Queen, is turned to the left.

THE LEOPARD'S HEAD

This famous mark, called in the Statute of 1363 the King's Mark, is the Hall-Mark showing that the spoon was made, or at least

MARKS ON OLD LONDON SPOONS

assayed, in London. The Leopard's Head, "Liberd's Heed," or "Catte's Face" as it is variously described, is actually the head of a lion passant guardant, in effect, a lion's full face, the error being believed to have arisen from a misunderstanding of the fact that the heraldic term *Leopart* in the old French, the language of the early English Statutes, means, not leopard but lion passant guardant, three such lions having constituted the arms of England ever since the days of Henry III.

This Leopard's Head, as already stated, should be found punched in the bowls of old London spoons of every sort, whatever their shape or their knop, right up to the coming of the Lobed-end spoon in the reign of Charles II.

Fortunate is the collector who acquires an early London spoon marked with the Leopard's Head Uncrowned enclosed within a plain or dotted circle—otherwise a ring of pellets in a circular stamp. He has obtained the rarest of all marked London spoons, one made before 1478, the approximate year in which the annual date-letter was adopted, and the Leopard's Head became ducally crowned or coronetted. It is now believed, however, that many spoons supposed to be fifteenth century London-made because of this uncrowned Leopard's Head are sixteenth century Shrewsbury spoons. [Vide Provincial spoons—Shrewsbury.]

Several Diamond-point or Spear-head spoons in the possession of famous English collectors, bearing the uncrowned Leopard's Head mentioned, are ascribed approximately to either 1400 or 1450, and are believed to have been made in London.

An Acorn-knop, sold at Christie's in 1905, and now in the famous Sir Charles Jackson collection, bears the uncrowned Leopard's Head without the dotted circle, and is ascribed to London, about the year 1390. This rare mark is shown on Plate V.

MARKS ON OLD LONDON SPOONS

The Leopard's Head changed its crown, its outline, its mane, its beard, its shield, even its tongue from time to time through the centuries, as is shown at a glance in the late Sir Charles Jackson's *English Goldsmiths and their Marks*, which is often described as the " Bible " of collectors of ancient English silver.

The often minute differences in the appearance of the Leopard's Head may seem trivial to the uninitiate, but they frequently materially assist the collector both in identifying and assessing the probable value of spoons, and also in distinguishing between, say, the Lombardic date-letter " B " (1479–80) of Edward IV and the closely similar Lombardic " B " (1519–20) of Henry VIII, the " D " of 1481–2, and the " D " of 1521–22, the " L " (1488–9) of Henry VII and the " L " (1528–9) of Henry VIII, the " N " of 1490–1, and the " N " of 1530–1, etc.

An earlier spoon, with certain exceptions, is much scarcer and more valuable than a later one of the same sort, and it is the minute differences in the various Leopard's Heads, date-letters and their shields, and so on, and even the changes made in his punch from time to time by the same maker, that, combined, enable the collector finally to fix the date of a spoon, particularly where one or more of the marks has become so worn or corroded as to be almost undecipherable.

THE MAKER'S MARK

The most human and individual of all the punches found on ancient silver spoons is the maker's mark. It was instituted by Statute in 1363, when it was enacted that every master goldsmith should have a mark of his own. This mark was originally, as was fitting in an age when comparatively few persons were able to read, a mere symbol termed, " the mark or sign of the worker." The early

OLD SILVER SPOONS OF ENGLAND

PLATE XVII

SEAL-TOPS AND APOSTLE ST. JOHN

THREE COMMONWEALTH EXAMPLES

HALL	STANDARD	MAKER	LETTER	DATE	INITIALS &c
LEOPARD'S HEAD CROWNED	LION PASSANT	WC	GT	1656	M T *on the button.*

Seal top spoon, pear shaped bowl, flattish hexagonal stem with baluster knob.

LEOPARD'S HEAD CROWNED	LION PASSANT	SV		1657	

Apostle spoon, St John with the cup of sorrow and hand raised in benediction, a star of eight rays on the nimbus, hexagonal stem, pear shaped bowl.

LEOPARD'S HEAD CROWNED	LION PASSANT	II		1658	

Seal top spoon, hexagonal stem. baluster knob, pear shaped bowl — Heavy and of large size. —

[L.C.]

PLATE XVII

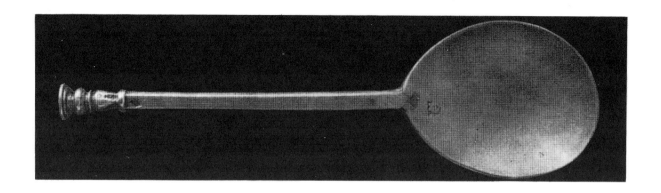

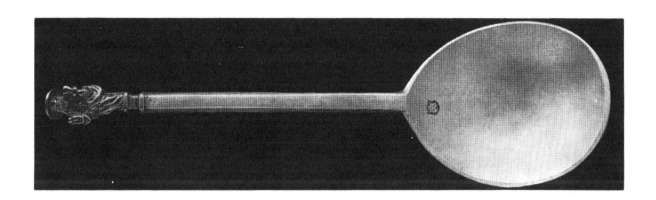

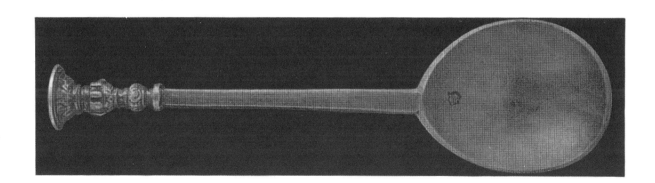

silversmiths, in some instances, used their shop-sign as their maker's mark, such as a key, fish, heart, bunch of grapes, eagle, falcon, or pair of compasses, the alternative shop-sign and maker's mark being sometimes an allusion to, or pun upon, the silversmith's name, such a device being termed a rebus.

A silversmith named Burd or Rose, for example, might, and did, adopt some sort of bird or a rose for both his shop sign and maker's mark, such symbols being perceived and remembered even by the illiterate.

The custom of using signs and symbols as shop-signs, instead of names, was to catch the eye, but it is fast disappearing in England, if not on the Continent.

The sole establishments where the custom not only survives but flourishes are the inns and public-houses, where a number of the older customers still find names difficult or impossible to read.

Examples of the old London goldsmith-bankers' signs are, or were, " The Golden Bottle," of Messrs. Hoare's bank, formerly in Cheapside; " The Three Squirrels," of Messrs. Gosling's Fleet Street bank; " The Marigold," of Child's bank in the same street, and " The Grasshopper," of Sir Thomas Gresham's establishment, afterwards occupied by Messrs. Martin, in Lombard Street. Sir Thomas' grasshopper appears to-day on the weather-vane of the Royal Exchange.

A number of these signs or symbols used as makers' marks will be encountered by the collector who acquires fifteenth or sixteenth century spoons. Here are a few examples, and the reigns in which they were used.

HENRY VII

A key was the maker's mark used on a Wrythen-knop of the date of 1488–9, in the Staniforth collection, and is shown on a Wrythen in this book. An upright cross within a circle (a cross pattée) was the maker's mark on Bishop Oldham's famous Owl-knops of 1506–7 at Corpus Christi College, Oxford.

HENRY VIII

A heart was the maker's mark on the famous Pudsey seal-top of 1525–6, on Bishop Fox's ball-knops of 1516–17 at Corpus Christi College, Oxford, on Lord Swaythling's six Apostles of 1524–15, and Archbishop Parker's Apostle of 1515–16 at Corpus Christi College, Cambridge.

The Eagle Displayed was the maker's mark on a Maidenhead of 1535–6, in the H. D. Ellis collection, and a Seal-top of 1572–3, belonging to the Armourers' Company.

A Sun was the mark on a Slipped-in-the-Stalk of 1523–4 in the Ellis collection.

A Sheaf of Arrows was the maker's mark in the complete set of Twelve Apostles and Master, dated 1536–7, which sold at Christie's for £4,900.

Letter S. A fringed or spiked capital letter S was an apparently popular maker's mark in the same reign. It appears on eleven Apostles of 1519–20 in the Staniforth collection, eight Apostles of 1527–8 from the Breadalbane collection, which sold at Christie's in May, 1926, for 460 guineas, and also on other Apostles of about this time that periodically reach the auction-room.

A Henry VIII Master spoon of 1530, also bearing this maker's mark, sold for one hundred guineas at the Charles James Toovey sale held at Christie's in February, 1926. This famous mark is shown on Plates VIII, IX and X.

OLD SILVER SPOONS OF ENGLAND

PLATE XVIII

SEAL-TOP, SLIPPED-IN-THE-STALK AND APOSTLE ST. BARTHOLOMEW

COMMONWEALTH, CHARLES I AND CHARLES II

HALL	STANDARD	MAKER	LETTER	DATE	INITIALS &c.
LEOPARD'S HEAD CROWNED	LION PASSANT	R W	B	1659	T·L on the button.

Seal top spoon, flattish hexagonal stem, baluster knob, pear shaped bowl.

LEOPARD'S HEAD CROWNED	LION PASSANT	I F	S	1641	N on the end.

Spoon, with hexagonal stem cut off obliquely at the end, pear shaped bowl.

LEOPARD'S HEAD CROWNED	LION PASSANT	W C	C	1660	on back of bowl

Apostle spoon, St. Bartholomew with a knife and a book, a dove on the nimbus, hexagonal stem, oval shaped bowl.

[L.C.]

PLATE XVIII

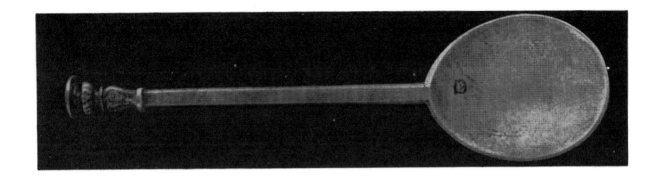

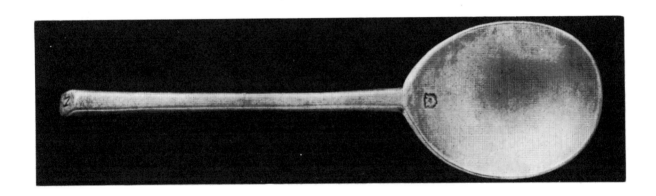

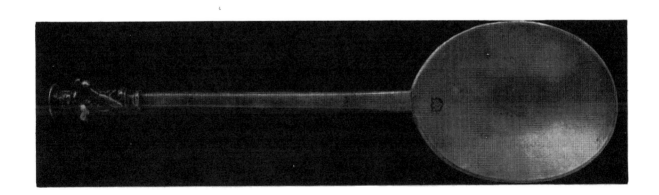

MARKS ON OLD LONDON SPOONS

ELIZABETH

A Bird's Claw was the maker's mark on both a set of Apostles dated 1566–7 at Corpus Christi College, Cambridge, and a Lion Sejant of 1560–1 in the H. D. Ellis collection.

Sun Rayed, otherwise "Sun In Splendour." This symbol, with a capital W in the centre, appears on an Apostle spoon of 1551–2 of the Innholders' Company.

Crossed Compasses, within a fringed circle, appear on an Apostle spoon of 1561–2 belonging to the Innholders' Company.

A Hand holding a Hammer is the maker's mark on another Apostle of 1569–70 in the possession of the same Company.

A Trefoil is the mark on a Seal-top, dated 1572–3, in the Ellis collection.

Escallop Shell. This is the maker's punch on an Apostle of 1578–9 in the Staniforth collection.

Crescent or Crescent Moon. This formed the major part of a number of Elizabethan spoon-makers' marks. Two crescents back to back, or a mill-rind, figure on Seal-tops of 1573–4 and 1575–6, belonging to the Armourers' Company. Two other Seal-tops in the same Company's collection, and dated 1586–7, bear respectively a Crescent enclosing the capital letter W and a Crescent beneath the capital letter T. A Crescent enclosing a star or mullet appears on other Armourers' Company's Seal-tops of 1590–1 and 1594–5.

Anchor. This appears on Seal-tops of 1592–3 and 1597–8 in the Armourers' Company collection.

The custom of using signs, symbols or emblems, unaccompanied by any initial letters, was rarely practised later than early in the reign

III

of James I. It was superseded by two letters, either the maker's initials or, from 1697 to 1719, the first two letters of his surname.

DATE-LETTERS

The list of London annual or date-letters, which were changed each year on May 19, before the Restoration, and on May 29 thereafter, can now be traced, with certain gaps in the early years, as far back as the year 1478–9 in the reign of Edward IV.

The list consists generally, in the case of London, of a series of twenty letters of the alphabet, which were repeated five times in each century in differing type, enclosed in shields of divers shapes.

The types of the alphabets used by the Goldsmiths' Company may be summarised as follows :—

1478 to 1497	Lombardic Letters.
1498 to 1517	Black Letter, Small.
1518–37	Lombardic and Roman Capitals.
1538–57	Lombardic and Roman Capitals.
1558–77	Black Letter, Small.
1578–97	Roman Capitals.
1598–1617	Lombardic.
1618–1637	Roman and Italics, Small.
1638–57	Court Hand.
1658–77	Black Letter Capitals.
1678–96	Black Letter Small.
1697–1715	Court Hand.
1716–35	Roman Capitals.
1736–55	Roman Small.
1756–75	Old English or Black Letter Capitals.
1776–95	Roman Letter Small.
1796–1815	Roman Capitals.
1816–35	Roman Small.
1836–55	Old English or Black Letter Capitals.

MARKS ON OLD LONDON SPOONS

This question of the marks on spoons and other silver is a voluminous subject in itself, and many excellent and adequate books are published to-day with which the present volume makes no attempt to compete.

These books range all the way from Mr. W. Chaffers' modest *Hallmarks on Gold and Silver Plate*, published at *7s. 6d.* ; Mr. W. J. Cripps' *Old English Plate*, which gives several thousand marks in facsimile ; and Mr. E. L. Lowes' *Chats on Old Silver*, right up to the late Sir Charles Jackson's *English Goldsmith's and their Marks*, which contains more than 13,000 makers' marks reproduced in facsimile, tables of date-letters and other marks employed by the London, provincial and other assay offices. There is no other book on marks to be compared with Sir Charles' work. It is only proposed here to touch on the question of marks as they affect spoons.

It is the date-letter which, more, perhaps, than any other mark, fixes the value of spoons. The absence of a date-letter, worn away maybe by centuries of cleaning and polishing, or possibly corroded out of all recognition by the carelessness of some dead and gone silver polisher in the home, frequently cuts almost in half the value of the spoon. The approximate date has then to be guessed by the variety of the spoon, the knop, the shape of the stem and bowl, and the other marks that remain.

Many small eighteenth and nineteenth century spoons, however, such as tea, snuff, coffee, salt, and the so-called small olive-spoons, which were actually used to strain tea, were not generally punched with either date-letter, Leopard's Head, Britannia figure or Sovereign's Head, their punches being often confined simply to the maker's mark and the Lion, or even the maker's mark alone.

CHAPTER XI

Provincial Spoons

Spoons made in Exeter, Lincoln, Norwich and York, the Provincial Spoons, most frequently encountered by collectors—The Town-marks described with examples bearing these marks—Chester, Hull, Leeds, Lewes, Leicester, Newcastle, Poole—The Shrewsbury Sixteenth Century Leopard's Head confused with the Fifteenth Century Leopard's Head of London—Salisbury, Sherborne and Taunton marks.

Unascribed English marks—Krishna, Vishnu, or Buddha-Knops, and the mystery of their makers and towns of origin.

MANY of the most interesting, earliest and most beautiful old English silver spoons were made in the provinces. They follow closely, with few exceptions, the forms of the old London spoons, display, in numbers of instances, every whit as fine metal and craftsmanship, and, in some cases, command even higher prices in the salerooms than their London prototypes. Date-letters, however, are absent, particularly in the earlier spoons, and their dates can consequently only be approximated.

Provincial spoons may be broadly divided into two classes, those whose marks have been identified as belonging to certain towns during certain periods, and those whose marks are still " unascribed," that is, have not been identified up to the present time, although they are declared to be unquestionably English spoons.

Silversmiths are known to have carried on their craft in Chester and Norwich as early as the thirteenth century, and at Exeter and York

PROVINCIAL SPOONS

100 years later. A number of provincial towns had their silversmiths producing spoons and other plate in the century preceding the Reformation.

Local guilds, made up of the master craftsmen, controlled the output of the provincial silversmiths in early times. The law provided in the fourteenth century that the spoons and other items of wrought gold and silver should be brought by a silversmith from the town concerned to London, there to be stamped with a Leopard's Head, the London assay mark.

The difficulties and dangers besetting such pilgrimages frequently caused this law to be disregarded, and a Statute of Richard II, in the latter part of the fourteenth century, therefore, provided that, thereafter, every goldsmith should put his own mark on his work, the local Mayors and Governors, and the local Master of the Mint, where such existed, stamping the mark of the borough or city on the spoon or other article, as the local Hall-mark.

Another statute in the first quarter of the fifteenth century gave definite authority to Bristow (Bristol), Coventry, Lincoln, "Newcastle-upon-Tine," Norwich, Salisbury and York, to have their distinctive "touches" or marks.

EXETER

The four principal towns most frequently identified with spoons encountered by the collector are Exeter, Lincoln, Norwich and York.

Johannes de Wewlingworth was a famous goldsmith, who carried on his craft in Exeter as early as 1327, and silversmiths in this city have left records of their skill in the form of many spoons dating from the middle of the sixteenth century and onwards.

The capital letter X, as a rule crowned, is the town-mark which, generally punched in the bowl, is most often met with in sixteenth century Exeter spoons, which range from Maidenheads and Apostles to Lion Sejants, Slipped-ends and Seal-tops.

The Tudor makers' marks include IONS in an oblong shield, being the mark of John Ions (Jones), ESTON, which figures on a Lion Sejant of 1592 in the Victoria and Albert Museum, OSBORN, which appears on a Maidenhead of 1600, and HERMAN on a Seal-top of the same year, both in the J. H. Walter collection.

The initials R.O. (Richard Osborn) in a heart-shaped shield appeared on an Apostle of 1600, acquired by Mr. Crichton. The initials I.L. (John Lavers) are the maker's marks which are punched on a Seal-top of about 1635 in Sir Edward Marshall-Hall's collection. An Exeter Acorn-knop, acquired by Mr. Crichton, and ascribed to the period between 1470 and 1500, has the crowned X in a shaped shield on the front of the stem near the bowl. A number of beautiful Puritans, Lobed-ends and Apostles, made in Exeter in the seventeenth century, have also survived, and frequently find their way into the sale-room, where they often realise high prices.

The arms of the city, per pale *gules* and *sable* a triple-towered castle, turreted, *or*, replaced the crowned X in 1700–1, whenceforward Exeter had its five marks, including the annual date-letter.

The characteristic early Exeter mark, the X crowned, is also shown on Plate XXIV.

Two Puritan spoons, bearing the Exeter mark, of about 1660, a Seal-top by Jasper Radcliffe, of Exeter, pricked "1648," another Seal-top by C. Eston, of Exeter, of about 1590, and an Exeter Apostle of St. Matthew of about 1640, were sold at the Breadalbane sale, held at Christie's in May, 1926. Exeter-made spoons are shown on Plates XXIV and XXV.

OLD SILVER SPOONS OF ENGLAND

PLATE XIX

PURITANS OR STUMP-TOPS

EARLY CHARLES II

HALL	STANDARD	MAKER	LETTER	DATE	INITIALS &c
LEOPARD'S HEAD CROWNED	LION PASSANT	I·I	JF	1663	

Spoon. small size. flat stem cut off straight at the end, egg shaped bowl.

HALL	STANDARD	MAKER	LETTER	DATE	INITIALS &c
LEOPARD'S HEAD CROWNED	LION PASSANT	I·I		1665	·F· I·E on back of stem

Spoon flat stem cut off straight at the end, oval bowl.

HALL	STANDARD	MAKER	LETTER	DATE	INITIALS &c
LEOPARD'S HEAD CROWNED	LION PASSANT	TS	J	1666	E❖E on the end of stem in front.

Spoon. flat stem cut off straight at the end. egg shaped bowl.

[L.C.]

PLATE XIX

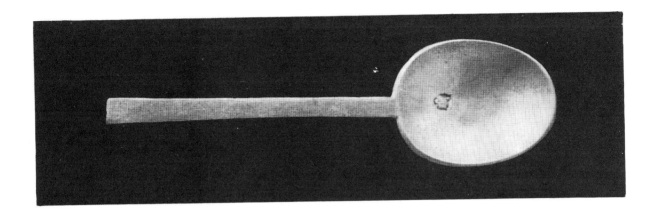

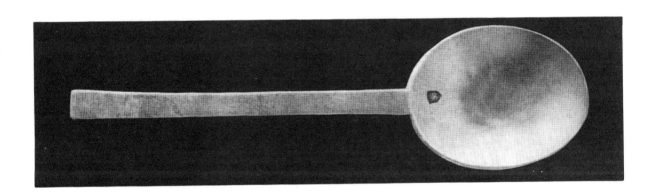

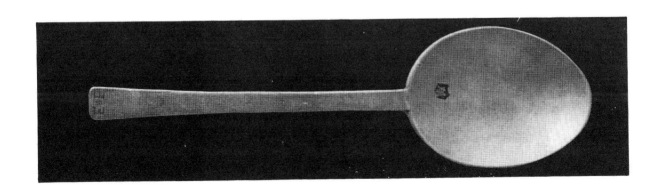

OLD SILVER SPOONS OF ENGLAND

" Aurifabers " or Goldsmiths flourished in Lincoln as far back as the twelfth century, and fine Lincoln-made spoons of most of the well-known varieties, dating from the time of Queen Elizabeth, frequently find their way into the sales rooms and dealers' show-cases.

The characteristic mark found punched in the bowls of the earlier Lincoln spoons is the Fleur-de-Lys, or so-called Prince of Wales' Feather. This Fleur-de-Lys refers to the Virgin Mary, whose emblem it is, and to whom the Cathedral Church of Lincoln was dedicated.

LINCOLN

Argent, on a cross gules, a Fleur-de-Lys or, are indeed the historic arms of Lincoln. The Fleur-de-Lys in the case of late seventeenth century Lincoln spoons, such as the Lobed-end and other flat-stemmed varieties, is found punched on the backs of the stems, frequently in company with the local maker's mark. Some of the Lincoln spoons bear one or more Fleurs-de-Lys, both in the bowl and on the back of the stem.

This Fleur-de-Lys appears sometimes in a plain or dotted circle, sometimes in a dotted lozenge, sometimes in a plain square, and sometimes without a shield at all. It is a mark which, in one form or another, is found on spoons from early Elizabethan times well into the reign of Queen Anne.

Moor's-Head

A small but very rare spoon, with a Moor's Head at the top of the stem and marked with the Fleur-de-Lys, with W as the Makers' mark, is in the Victoria & Albert Museum and is ascribed to the middle of the 16th Century. This spoon, which is assigned to Lincoln, is shown on Plate XXV.

PROVINCIAL SPOONS

Goldsmiths were working in Norwich as early as the late thirteenth century, and many of the Elizabethan Norwich-made spoons which find their way into the market to-day are every whit as fine as the best London-made spoons of the period.

Peter Peterson, a descendant of one of the Dutch colonists who settled in Norwich, and who was elected a freeman in 1553, making spoons and other plate for half a century and, dying at the age of eighty-four, was one of the most famous of the Norwich goldsmiths of Elizabeth's age. The Sun in Splendour and the Orb and Cross are variously ascribed as his maker's mark.

It may be mentioned that no authentic example of a Norwich Apostle spoon is known, and that a number of so-called Norwich Apostle spoons of the first half of the seventeenth century, which are punched in the bowl with the crowned rose, are in reality Dutch spoons.

A Castle over a Lion is the town-mark generally found on Norwich spoons bearing date-letters from 1565–6 to 1580–1, with a Crowned Rose, or another form of Castle over a Lion, on later spoons up to about 1697.

York was, in mediæval times, the most important provincial city in England, York-made spoons being mentioned in wills and inventories as early as 1366.

One of the earliest examples of these spoons known to be in existence is in the collection of Mr. Harvey Clark. It has the usual fig-shaped bowl, with a tapering

OLD SILVER SPOONS OF ENGLAND

PLATE XX

SHOWING CHANGES IN BOWL AND STEM IN THE MIDDLE AND LATTER PART OF SEVENTEENTH CENTURY

(1) SLIPPED-IN-THE-STALK. LONDON, 1651–2 (EARLY COMMONWEALTH).

(2) PURITAN. ABOUT 1660. ? NORWICH (EARLY CHARLES II).

(3) PURITAN OR SQUARE-END. LONDON, 1665–6 (DUG UP IN CHELSEA). (EARLY CHARLES II).

(4) AND (5) LOBED-END. LONDON, 1679–80 (LATE CHARLES II), SHOWING DECORATED STEM AND BOWL AND RAT-TAIL.

[V. AND A. M.]

PLATE XX

stem surmounted by an ornamental Gothic finial. It is ascribed to about 1490–1500.

It bears, stamped in the bowl, the famous ancient York town-mark, the curious " halfe leopard head and half flowre-de-luyce " (Fleur-de-Lys).

This curious mark is found on York spoons right down to 1631, and, from 1560, both date-letters and makers' marks are frequently added.

The " halfe leopard head," however, on spoons from 1632 to 1698 is replaced by a half rose crowned.

The town-mark was again changed in 1700 to a cross charged with five lions passant.

The ancient half-and-half mark, unparalleled in Provincial town-marks, is shown on the curious York-made " In Memoriam " or " Death " spoon on Plate XXIV.

A York Seal-top of 1560—for many of the York spoons bear date-letters—with an octagonal seal and gilt bowl, and X as the maker's mark, sold at the Breadalbane sale at Christie's in May, 1926, for fourteen guineas.

Other town-marks are occasionally encountered on ancient English spoons.

Goldsmiths were established in Chester from the thirteenth century, and their assay office survives to this day.

CHESTER

Few Chester spoons earlier than the end of the seventeenth century are known to collectors.

A Chester Lobed-end of 1686–90 with (1) the initials A.P. conjoined (Alexander Pulford) in a shaped shield as the maker's mark, (2) the, Chester town-mark—three garbes surmounted by a sword in pale, (3)

121

a plume of three feathers encircled with a coronet in a plain shield—the badge of the Prince of Wales, who is also Earl of Chester, and (4) a small black letter "a" in a shield, was sold with two others, made by Nathaniel Bullen, of Chester, for fourteen guineas the three, at the Breadalbane sale.

Few spoons made in Hull in the sixteenth and seventeenth centuries are encountered by collectors.

A Seal-top ascribed to about 1587 at Trinity House, Hull, bears the capital letter H as the town mark in a square shield, and the initials I.C. (James Carlille) above a small animal—possibly a sheep—the whole in a shaped shield, as the maker's mark. Another Seal-top at Trinity House, ascribed to about 1635, has two town marks, the H already described, and *three ducal coronets in pale*, the town arms adopted as the town-mark in the seventeenth century. The maker's mark is R.R. (Robert Robinson) below a mullet in a plain shield.

A Hull Lobed-end of about 1697, acquired by Mr. Crichton, has K.M. (Katherine Mangy) in a decorative shield as the maker's mark.

LEEDS

The mark of the Golden Fleece, which appears on two late seventeenth century Lobed-ends in the J. H. Walter collection, is believed to be that of Leeds, this badge of the Golden Fleece figuring in the ancient town arms.

LEWES

The adapted ancient Lewes, Sussex, town-mark, a shield with a lion rampant in the upper right-hand corner, and black and white squares, in lay language, on the rest of the shield, was used by the local goldsmiths as their town-mark. The town mark's official

122

description is "*checky (or and azure)*" on "*a canton sinister gules a lion rampant, or.*"

It appears on Seal-tops of about 1590 in the H. D. Ellis and J. H. Walter collections and other rare early seventeenth century spoons. A small Seal-top in the British Museum, assigned to the late sixteenth century, bears this mark, which is described as of "the arms of Warren or of the town of Lewes."

LEICESTER

The cinquefoil of Leicester's ancient coat of arms is found on scarce sixteenth and seventeenth century Leicester-made spoons, such as the late seventeenth century Maidenhead in the J. H. Walter collection, and several Seal-tops of the early seventeenth century in the H. D. Ellis collection.

NEWCASTLE

No spoons with a definite Newcastle mark have been encountered earlier than of the reign of Queen Anne.

A Lobed-end with the Newcastle date-letter for 1704–5, bearing the Newcastle mark—Three Castles— two castles over a third—in a shield shaped at the top—the Britannia Figure, the Lion's Head erased and Sh over a Mullet (Robert Shrive) as the maker's mark, was acquired by Mr. Crichton. This is one of the earliest known Newcastle spoons.

POOLE

An Escallop-shell within a ring of pellets, the whole in a circular shield, appears on a Seal-top of about 1540, acquired by Mr. Crichton, with R.S. as the maker's mark. This spoon is believed to have been made in Poole, three escallops in chief occurring in the arms of the Borough.

123

PROVINCIAL SPOONS

Both an Apostle and a Seal-top of about 1620 in the Sir E. Marshall-Hall collection bear other varieties of escallop, and are also assigned to Poole.

SALISBURY

Seven silver Seal-top spoons dug up together during excavations at Netherhampton, Wilts, and now in the King Edward wing of the British Museum (Treasure Trove) have led to a number of marks being tentatively ascribed to Salisbury.

One of these spoons, which has "1596" pricked or pounced on the seal or button, has, as its mark, the letters TR conjoined, in a dotted circle, a mark very similar to one frequently ascribed to Truro. A second Seal-top, pricked "1629" on the seal, has the letters FR conjoined, within a plain circle.

Two others, one pricked "1596," and the other "1621," have an arrangement of dots or pellets within a dotted circle, somewhat similar to the mark illustrated in connection with Sherborne.

A fifth, pricked "1621," has the single letter I between two pellets, the whole in a plain circle, a sixth, pricked "1629," CB conjoined, within a plain circle, and a seventh, pricked "1621," an H in a shaped shield.

These may possibly be the marks of goldsmiths of Salisbury, which was appointed as early as 1423 to have a mark of its own, but the present evidence is vague.

SHREWSBURY

Silver spoons were made in Shrewsbury as far back as the Middle Ages, and a Statute of 1300, re-enacted in subsequent Acts, ordaining

OLD SILVER SPOONS OF ENGLAND

PLATE XXI

LOBED-ENDS OR TREFOIL-TOPS

LATE CHARLES II

HALL	STANDARD	MAKER	LETTER	DATE	INITIALS &c
LEOPARD'S HEAD CROWNED	LION PASSANT	AK	S	1675	Arms of Kings College, Cambridge and date, on back of stem

Spoon, egg shaped bowl triple lined rat's tail, plain flat stem with trefoil top. Found in the Cam.

LEOPARD'S HEAD CROWNED	LION PASSANT	AK	1677	P R*M on back of stem

Spoon, egg shaped bowl with triple lined rat's tail and chased acanthus leaf, flat trefoil scroll top with leafage & cherub's head ornament in front.

HALL	STANDARD	MAKER	LETTER	DATE	INITIALS &c
LEOPARD'S HEAD CROWNED	LION PASSANT	EH	P	1682	P*B on the back of stem.

Spoon, oval bowl with rat's tail and chased design on back as sketched, flat stem chased ornamental trefoil top.

[L.C.]

PLATE XXI

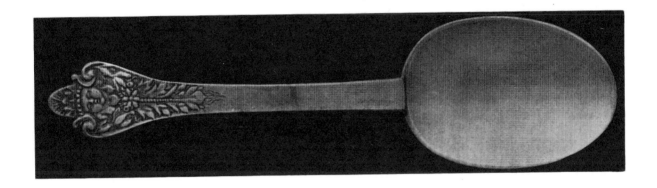

the mark of the Leopard's Head (*azure, three leopards heads, or,* being the Shrewsbury arms) has led to some confusion among collectors between early Shrewsbury and early London spoons.

A number of spoons punched in the bowl with the uncrowned Leopard's Head, are erroneously ascribed to London for the reason that closely similar marks have been found in the bowls of spoons made in London before 1478—in, or about, which year the date-letter was first introduced. Two of the authenticated London uncrowned Leopards' Heads in a dotted circle are shown on Plate V.

It is now considered probable that the majority of spoons bearing the uncrowned Leopard's Head are not fifteenth century London productions at all, but sixteenth century Shrewsbury spoons.

The collector, however, may console himself in either contingency that, whether his spoon be London fifteenth or Shrewsbury sixteenth, he is the possessor of a great rarity.

Little can be stated with any certainty concerning Shrewsbury marks.

A roll of Shrewsbury goldsmiths from 1465 to 1695 has been compiled, but few authenticated examples of their spoons and other wares appear to have survived.

SHERBORNE

A number of pellets or dots in a circular shield constitute the mark found punched in the bowl of many late sixteenth and early seventeenth century seal-tops, which find their way from time to time into the shops and sale rooms.

The marks are believed to be those of Richard Orenge, a goldsmith of Sherborne, Dorsetshire, who was churchwarden at Charlton, both in 1585 and 1596, and whose will was proved in 1606.

PROVINCIAL SPOONS

The rebus T on tun (or cask) is the famous Taunton mark—generally in a circular shield—frequently encountered by collectors of seventeenth century, and particularly of Lobed-end, spoons. An Apostle spoon acquired by Mr. Crichton, and ascribed to about 1645, bears this town-mark and the letters S.R. conjoined as the maker's mark, and another Apostle, engraved " 1689," the same-town mark in a shaped shield, with I.S. in a shaped shield, and punched twice, as the maker's mark. A flat-stemmed spoon, with a lobed end and pricked " 1682," in the Victoria and Albert Museum, bears the same town-mark in a circular shield, with T.D. punched twice, as the maker's mark.

UNASCRIBED ENGLISH MARKS

Old English spoons bearing marks unaccompanied by any definitely authenticated town-marks are currently spoken of as having " unascribed " marks.

They offer a rich and highly interesting field to collectors, particularly to those of modest means.

They likewise present pretty little problems in fixing the approximate dates and periods in which they were made, for the collector has here often to judge solely by his knowledge of the style of knop, stem and bowl, assisted, although in some cases, hindered, by the dates frequently engraved, pounced or scratched on some portion of the spoon.

Sir Charles Jackson suggested that many of these marks were possibly punched by pewterers on spoons made for their own use, and his book on marks, already referred to, contains several hundreds of

OLD SILVER SPOONS OF ENGLAND

PLATE XXII

LOBED-ENDS OR TREFOIL-TOPS

JAMES II, AND WILLIAM AND MARY

HALL	STANDARD	MAKER	LETTER	DATE	INITIALS &c
LEOPARD'S HEAD CROWNED	LION PASSANT			1686	

Spoon, very small, egg shaped rat's tail bowl, plain flat stem with leaf top. (Probably used for snuff)

HALL	STANDARD	MAKER	LETTER	DATE	INITIALS &c
LEOPARD'S HEAD CROWNED	LION PASSANT	WM		1688	RF on front of stem MG on back of stem

Spoon, oval bowl quintuple lined rat's tail, plain flat stem trefoil top.

HALL	STANDARD	MAKER	LETTER	DATE	INITIALS &c
LEOPARD'S HEAD CROWNED	LION PASSANT	LC		1689	RP on front of stem

Spoon, small size, oval bowl triple lined rat's tail, plain flat stem trefoil top.

[L.C.]

PLATE XXII

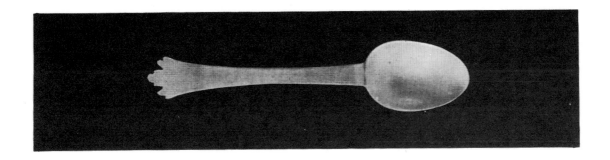

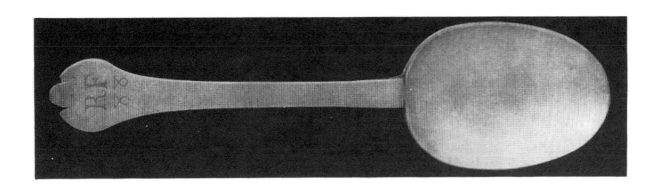

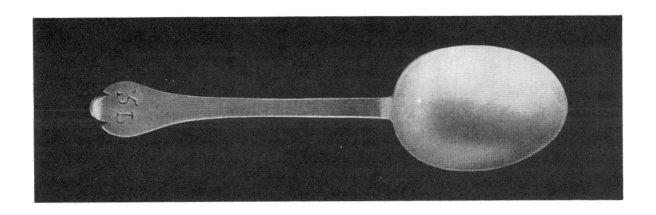

PROVINCIAL SPOONS

these mysterious punches with their approximate dates. It is also possible that they were made by silversmiths, particularly spoonmakers, for their own use.

The unascribed marks, which consist of initials, or curious symbols, or both, are found frequently on beautiful specimens of unmistakably ancient English spoons of almost all varieties and periods, ranging from a Wrythen-knop of about 1500 in Sir Charles' collection, to a George II Marrow-scoop in Windsor Castle.

Beautiful old English spoons, bearing only unascribed marks, include Diamond-points, Maidenheads, Lion Sejants, Finial-tops, Apostles and Masters, Seal-tops, Baluster-tops, Buddha-knops, and other terminal figures, Horse-hoof knops, Puritans, Lobed-ends, Shield-top or Waved-ends and Georgian Rat-tails.

A number of famous collections contain examples of these homeless " unascribed."

These spoons are, other things being equal, the cheapest of all marked specimens to acquire. They are still cheaper, if unmentioned in Jackson.

A fully-marked London late Elizabethan Seal-top in excellent condition, for example, might cost anywhere from £15 to £25. A similar spoon, with provincial marks of about the same time, might be had for £10, and a " provincial unascribed " mentioned in Jackson for £7.

A " provincial unascribed " not mentioned in Jackson, with the sole mark, say, a crowing cock within a circular shield, pricked with two sets of initials and the date " 1594 " pounced on the top of the seal, might be obtained on the other hand for three or four guineas, although in fine condition, with a lovely bowl, and showing in half a dozen ways that it was made not later than the end of the sixteenth century.

129

OLD SILVER SPOONS OF ENGLAND

The collector in acquiring it would here be put on his mettle in judging its period. The form of the seal-and-baluster, the shape of the stem, the narrowness of the neck of the bowl, the broadness of the base of the bowl, the "shoulder" on the bowl, the "dip" of the bowl after it left the stem, the fact that a bird, unaccompanied by any letter or letters, was used as the sole mark— all these clues would combine to lead him to the approximate date of the specimen, independent of the pricking.

BUDDHA- KRISHNA- OR VISHNU-KNOPS

This mysterious variety of provincial unascribed, which is frequently referred to as merely a "terminal figure" spoon, is topped by a somewhat grotesque figure supposed to represent Buddha, Krishna, or Vishnu.

These are rare provincial spoons, whose makers, or towns of origin or assay, cannot be stated definitely.

They belong to the period between 1600 and 1655, and are said to have had some connection originally with the founding of the East India Company in 1600 and the opening up of commerce with the East.

Several examined by the author, including one at South Kensington attributed to about the year 1630, have what appears to be a bunch of grapes stamped in the bowl, and on the back of the stem (*a*) a small quatrefoil, and (*b*) the initials R.C. with a mullet or star between, in a roughly rectangular, but somewhat shaped shield. Another, submitted to the author, of about 1600, has IS in monogram, within a shaped shield, stamped in the bowl as its only mark.

An example in the collection of Sir E. Marshall-Hall, K.C., ascribed to about 1640, is punched with CR. in monogram, with a mullet above

PROVINCIAL SPOONS

a pellet on the left of the monogram, and a mullet on the right, the whole in a lozenge-shaped shield. Some of these curiously-knopped spoons have what appears to be a crudely-designed Fleur-de-lys punched in the bowl. This has led to their being wrongly ascribed as having been made in Lincoln. A comparison of the two marks will at once reveal the distinction.

A spoon, officially described as a " Buddha " spoon, inscribed with the date " 1637 " and, for marks, a bunch of grapes stamped in the bowl, with H.C. (? R.C.), and a quatrefoil *incuse* on the back of the stem, the gift of Thomas, Earl of Arundel and Surrey, was shown by the Mercers' Company at the London Livery Companies' Exhibition at South Kensington in the summer of 1926.

Similar effigies, although of course on a much larger scale, figure in Jacobean and late Elizabethan architecture.

These spoons realise from £20 upwards apiece.

Illustration on Plate XXV.

131

CHAPTER XII

SOME SUGGESTIONS TO WOULD-BE COLLECTORS OF EARLY OLD ENGLISH SPOONS

Collecting old Brass and Pewter Spoons as a method of training—Most ancient Silver Spoons have counterparts in base metal—Beginning to collect with Georgian silver and then working backwards—What the South Kensington Museum and Christie's sales' rooms can teach the collector—The best book on silver marks—Two sorts of collectors, the well-to-do and those of modest means—Their acquisition methods compared—Bargains at the Breadalbane sale—The student collector and the romance of Old Silver Spoons—The fear of forgeries—Early Silver Spoons not for daily use—Advantages of the Spoon-stand—Cleaning old Silver Spoons—De Lamerie's advice.

A FEW suggestions to would-be collectors of old English silver spoons may not be out of place here. Budding collectors not many years ago used to begin by collecting ancient pewter and latten (brass) spoons, which, with certain exceptions, follow closely the shapes and periods of the silver varieties. (Latten is derived from the old French word *laton*, a mixed mediæval metal made of copper and zinc, and not practically distinguishable from brass. Shakespeare, who is reported to have been godfather to one of Ben Jonson's children, on being asked after the christening why he seemed so preoccupied, replied, according to Hone's *Every Day Book* : " Ben, I have been considering a great while what should be the fittest gift for me to bestow upon my godchild, and I have resolved it at last." " I prithee, what ? " said

132

SUGGESTIONS TO COLLECTORS

Ben. "I'faith, Ben," replied Shakespeare, "I'll give him a dozen good latten spoons, and thou shalt translate them!")

Silver Apostles, Acorn-knops, Wrythens, Strawberry-knops or Fruitlets, Maidenheads, Slipped-in-the-Stalks, Lion Sejants, Seal-and-Baluster-tops, Horsehoof-knops, Puritans, Lobed-ends and Rat-tails, all have their counterparts in ancient brass or pewter.

These base-metal spoons are considerably coarser than the silver varieties, and their times of making can only be approximated owing to the absence of date-letters, and, indeed, every mark other than the maker's mark or "touch." They thus used to offer valuable training in the periods of spoons independent of their marks.

They could be acquired for only a fraction of the cost of silver spoons, and served, in many instances, as a useful introduction to the collection of spoons in the finer metal.

Both old pewter and brass English spoons, alas, are to-day much rarer than silver, and a large proportion of the so-called ancient base-metal spoons now offered for sale in the antique shops are either of Continental origin or modern English copies of the old spoons, some of them so cunningly forged to represent age as to deceive anyone but an expert.

The dealers themselves, in many instances, state frankly that they do not profess to say if the spoon is an old one or a copy.

It is doubtful indeed if there are twenty authentic ancient English base metal spoons on sale anywhere in London to-day, and the provinces can offer very few more, judging by the experiences of ardent collectors who have scoured the country for them. Both the London and the Guildhall Museums, however, possess fine collections, and the British and Victoria and Albert Museums a few.

The modern amateur collectors, particularly those of modest means, frequently begin by collecting spoons of the time of George III or

SUGGESTIONS TO COLLECTORS

George IV for domestic use, work backwards to George II, George I, and Anne, and thence to the romantic seventeenth, and, to many, even more romantic, sixteenth century.

The general rule is that the earlier the spoon the higher the price, because of its greater rarity and antiquity.

A London Apostle spoon of the time of Henry VIII, in fine condition, with excellent marks, and surmounted by the figure, say, of St. Matthew, may realise as much as fifty guineas, but a similar Apostle of Charles I in equally good condition and well marked, less than one half that sum, and one of William and Mary's reign less than one quarter.

A similar statement applies to other spoons, although there is no hard-and-fast rule.

The collector who genuinely loves old silver, and particularly old silver spoons, because of the intimate, personal, individual, qualities associated with their former use, would be well advised to visit the Victoria and Albert Museum at South Kensington, which houses, in its silver section proper, and its Loan Court, probably the finest collection of old English silver spoons in the world.

Virtually every variety of old English silver spoon in existence to-day, with few exceptions, is here represented in the glass cases, many of the examples being the only ones of their kind known, and all can be studied at leisure.

The would-be collector will thus be able to discover his personal prejudices and preferences, and will learn the appearance and general " look " of an authentic spoon.

He will likewise soon acquire that invaluable part of the collector's knowledge, the ability to tell the period in which the spoon was wrought and often its town of origin by its knop, the shape of its handle, the form

PLATE XXIII

LOBED-ENDS OR TREFOIL-TOPS

QUEEN ANNE, AND WILLIAM AND MARY

HALL	STANDARD	MAKER	LETTER	DATE	INITIALS &c
LION'S HEAD ERASED	BRITANNIA			1704	

Spoon, flat trefoil top stem engraved in leafage and scroll ornamentation both sides, oval bowl with rat's tail and engraved leaf design as sketched.

LEOPARD'S HEAD CROWNED	LION PASSANT			1691	

Tea spoon, flat stem with leafage engraving and trefoil top, oval rat's tail lined bowl engraved with leaf ornament.

LEOPARD'S HEAD CROWNED	LION PASSANT			1692	

Spoon, flat stem, chased scroll & trefoil top, oval bowl with rat's tail & chased ornament as sketched. —Fine example.—

MG on back
1693 of
stem

[L.C.]

PLATE XXIII

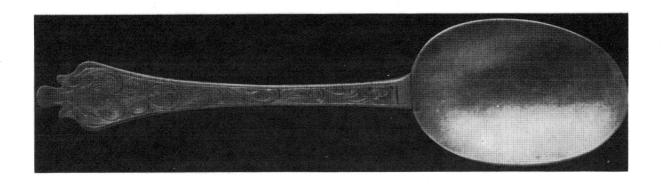

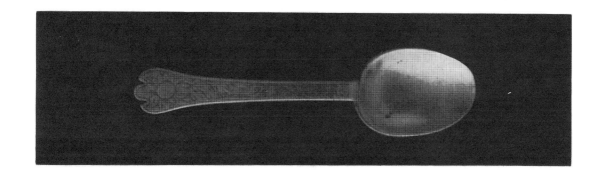

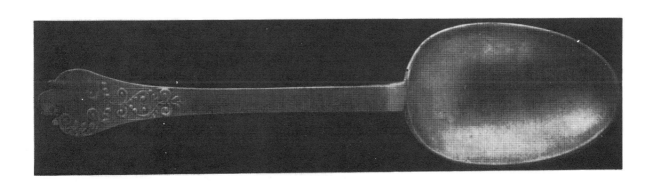

of the bowl or spoon-self, and the town or other mark punched in the bowl of most spoons of between 1500 and 1660.

This will enable him to distinguish between English and foreign spoons of similar shapes, and to know a " find " when he sees it, sometimes in the most unlooked-for places, both at home and abroad.

The Museum also contains a wonderful art library, including books on old silver, which is open to the public.

The collector should also make a point of attending the periodic sales of old silver spoons at Christie's and elsewhere, duly advertised in *The Times, Daily Telegraph, Morning Post*, and other newspapers.

The spoons are generally available for inspection for one or two days preceding the auction, and the collector may here not only see, but handle, the articles.

He will learn here the " feel " of an authentic spoon, the silky smoothness of the ancient silver worn by centuries of use and cleaning, the curious " pitting " caused by the action of time, and also, frequently by interment through long ages beneath the soil, for many of the fine specimens that change hands to-day have been discovered all over the country during excavations.

A fragment of a beautiful Maidenhead of the time of Henry VIII, with a deep rent in the middle of the bowl where the excavator's pick had probably caught it, but with the beautiful little image at the top of the stem intact, and retaining its original lovely gilding, both stem and bowl showing the characteristic fine dark patina and encrustation of centuries of burial, recently came into the Author's possession.

The " pitting " effect of this burial is clearly shown on the inside of the bowl of the small Lobed-end illustrated on Plate XXVI.

The collector during these inspections will also, if he is interested and anxious to learn, quickly acquire the dealer's facility of testing in a second with his thumb whether the base or other portion of a much-worn spoon has been hammered out to give it the appearance of its original shape. The edges of such spoons have a sharpness, which is readily distinguished from the genuine wear of a very thin bowled spoon, and it should be borne in mind that many of the provincial spoons were made thin for the twofold reason of lightness and economy. The bowls of both London and provincial spoons of the troublous times of Charles I, in particular, were also frequently made very light.

A hammered-out bowl materially depreciates the value of a spoon in the eyes of dealers and discerning collectors alike. A handle or other part of a spoon that has been broken and mended is approved still less.

A safe rule for an owner is to leave a worn or damaged spoon in its original condition, whether good, bad or indifferent—apart, of course from cleaning it, and some collectors even refuse to have this done.

An amateur collector known to the author unwisely sent away a Puritan spoon to have the curled-up side of the bowl hammered out. It was returned to him hammered out, but with the already faint Leopard's Head in the bowl completely burnished away, and the spoon, when subsequently put up to auction, failed to secure a single bid. The bowl appeared to be pin-new, although, of course, this was not the case.

The regilding of the knop of a spoon, where necessary, is the one thing considered permissible, and many collectors prefer to leave even this untouched.

The collector will also learn to note if the spoon has been tampered with at the junction of the stem and knop, and whether the knop is original or a later substitute.

The serious collector should also obtain a copy of Sir Charles Jackson's *English Goldsmiths and their Marks*. He may indemnify himself for the three guineas which the book costs in a single bargain

OLD SILVER SPOONS OF ENGLAND

PLATE XXIV

PROVINCIALS: EXETER ELIZABETHAN SEAL-TOP AND LION SEJANT, AND CURIOUS CHARLES II YORK SPOON

OFFICE	COUNTERMARK	MAKER	LETTER	DATE	INITIALS &c
EXETER	NIL	NIL	NIL	CIRCA 1572	*John Carews Legasey to R Æ on back of stem.*

Seal top spoon, gilt, hexagonal stem, baluster knob, pear shaped bowl. — Of stout make. —

EXETER	NIL	YEDS	I	CIRCA 1572	*I B on back of bowl.*

Spoon, pear shaped bowl, hexagonal stem surmounted by a lion sejant. — In good condition. —

YORK	NONE	IP	E	1661	**LIVE TO DIE** *on front of stem* **DIE TO LIVE** *on back of do.*

Spoon, shaped flat stem with engraved ornamentation both front & back, egg shaped bowl with V:B:. *on the back.*

on front at top. — *on back at top*

[L.C.]

PLATE XXIV

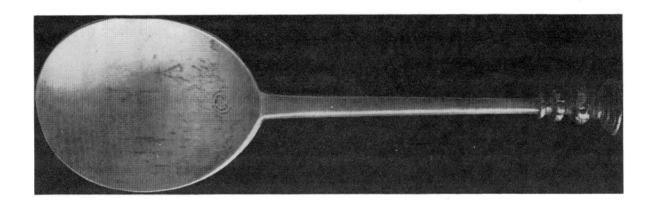

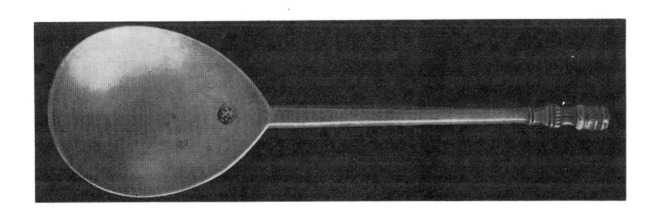

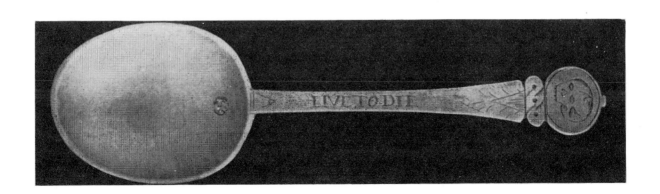

acquired by the expert information of marks contained in the volume.

There are two sorts of collectors of old English silver spoons.

One is the collector, frequently with considerable means at his disposal, who insists on acquiring only spoons in perfect condition, with full clear marks, London marks for preference, showing the precise year in which the spoon was made, another condition of his purchase being often that the marks are specifically mentioned in Sir Charles Jackson's book.

The dealers cater largely for collectors of this sort who, as likely as not, are buying as an investment, certain that their spoons will yield them a good profit when the time comes to sell. The beauty of particular bowls, stems and knops, is a secondary consideration to most of this class of collector.

The other sort of collector is the enthusiast, who cares more for beautiful specimens than for fine marks, and, indeed, would find costly examples quite beyond the reach of his purse.

He recognises the period of spoons almost at sight, conjectures "Probably about 1550," whenever he catches a glimpse of an octagonal seal-top, and knows how a "shoulder" found on the "stalk end" of a narrow-necked, pear-shaped bowl, with an unusually broad lip, points almost infallibly to a sixteenth century specimen, even in the absence of marks, which have either worn away with centuries of rubbing or else have never been punched at all, possibly because the specimen was made in some West of England town which could not boast a Hall-Mark.

He cons, with the aid of a magnifying glass, every pin-point of the surface of the spoon he has bought with an instinct for its possible rarity and interest, carefully examines any pricking or pouncing of dates and

139

initials for confirmation of its probable date, puzzles over any fragments of worn marks, and studiously consults his Jackson until he has solved, to his own satisfaction at least, the pretty problem of the spoon's antecedents.

He frequently finds that the despised spoon he has purchased for a mere song is to him a veritable treasure.

If he has bought wisely and cheaply he, too, can be assured of being able to sell again at a modest profit, or, at all events at little loss, should the need arise.

The especial field of this collector is the spoons known as " unascribed " provincial, which, as already stated, cannot at present be ascribed to any particular English town or their maker's mark identified, although their English origin and form are undisputed. It is always possible, of course, that sooner or later they will be identified, thanks to further research.

The difference in the points of view of these two principal varieties of collectors was strikingly emphasised anew at the sale of the Marquis of Breadalbane's collection of London and provincial spoons at Christie's on May 12th, 1926, the auctioneer announcing the calling off of the General Strike just before the early English spoons came under the hammer.

The first of these early English spoons offered was one of the noted Wrythen-knops. This spoon was immediately the object of considerable competition among the famous London dealers present, for this type of spoon is very rare. It was a fifteenth century specimen, little used and in fine condition, with good marks showing it had been made in London between the spring of 1488 and the spring of 1489.

It was just the sort of spoon which would appeal to a rich collector as an investment.

SUGGESTIONS TO COLLECTORS

The price of it, as mentioned elsewhere, rose to one hundred guineas before it was knocked down at that figure to a prominent Bond Street dealer.

The next item in the catalogue was described as " another spoon very similar. Maker's mark I B in a dotted circle."

The auctioneer, in this case, had difficulty in securing any opening offer at all for the spoon, although all those present, dealers and private collectors alike, had an opportunity of inspecting and handling it, both before and during the sale.

It was a beautiful, homely old specimen with a fine clearly defined wrythen-knop, a well-worn stem or stele, and an even more worn, although lovely, broad thin pear-shaped bowl, the silver slightly slit, split or torn, at the lip of the bowl. Nothing, however, was missing; the small contusions on the inside of the bowl giving the impression that it had been dug up.

The spoon had no other punches than the mark in the bowl.

The first sort of collector already described, and the dealers who catered to his wishes, had no interest in the spoon, for the bowl was slightly split at the base, and its only " touch " was one of the " unascribed."

Here was the opportunity for the second sort of collector mentioned. He became its proud and surprised possessor for the modest sum of six guineas. A reference to Jackson showed that this spoon was specifically mentioned in the famous book, and, indeed, has the place of honour among the early " Scottish unascribed " marks. The " Breadalbane " punch, in this instance, was absent from the stem.

It was assigned in Jackson to about the year 1500, the I B being possibly the ancient mark of Inverness. It is now in the National collection at the Victoria and Albert Museum, to which all good collectors should give the refusal of their rarest and choicest pieces. It is shown on Plate IV.

The same collector, who for years had coveted a Lion Sejant because of its wonderful knop, but had been deterred by the £35 asked for even a provincial specimen, had his second opportunity a few minutes later when two Provincial Lion Sejants were put up to auction together.

One of these had certain " Provincial unascribed " marks attributed to the period between 1570–80, and its bowl was somewhat marred by having been trimmed at the lip portion, but the beautifully gilded lion knop, familiar to collectors of Exeter Lion Sejants in particular, was perfect, the slim hexagonal stem was clearly stamped thrice at the back with the R.M. of the unknown maker's initials, in a shaped shield, and the mysterious symbol, which looks like a scarab above a swallow, was clearly punched in the bowl.

The other Lion Sejant had no marks at all, if the Breadalbane punch on the back of the stem be excepted. It was in perfect condition, however, with a lovely, characteristic, little-worn, Tudor bowl.

Now, the essence of a Lion Sejant to many private collectors, lies in the knop, frequently a little masterpiece of the ancient silversmith's art.

Both these knops were perfect, and both were different. The collector realised his ambition when the spoons were knocked down to him for seven guineas the pair. The unmarked example is shown on Plate XXVI.

A beautiful little Slipped-in-the-Stalk of about 1640, in perfect condition, but again unmarked, was acquired by another collector at the same sale for two-and-a-half guineas. A similar spoon with full London marks, but indistinguishable at a few inches distance from the anonymous specimen, would cost at least £15.

OLD SILVER SPOONS OF ENGLAND

PLATE XXV

FIVE INTERESTING PROVINCIAL SPOONS

(1) APOSTLE, ? ST. PHILIP, EXETER, ABOUT 1630. TOWN-MARK X CROWNED, WITHIN SHAPED SHIELD. MAKER'S MARK I.R. WITH FOLIAGE BETWEEN, AND RADCLIFF IN A PLAIN SHIELD (JASPER RADCLIFFE). [L.C.]

(2) LION SEJANT, EXETER, ? 1589. TOWN-MARK X CROWNED WITHIN DOTTED CIRCLE. MAKER'S MARK, ESTON, WITHIN DOTTED RECTANGULAR SHIELD (C. ESTON).

(3) TERMINAL FIGURE, KRISHNA-, VISHNU- OR BUDDHA-KNOP. DATE ABOUT 1630. INSCRIBED "1652." UNASCRIBED MARK IN BOWL, A BUNCH OF GRAPES. UNASCRIBED MARKS, ON BACK OF STEM, R.C., WITH A MULLET BETWEEN, IN SHAPED SHIELD, AND A QUATREFOIL.

(4) MOOR'S HEAD. ? LINCOLN. DATE ABOUT 1550.
MARKS: FLEUR-DE-LYS IN BOWL AND W ON STEM.

(5) ACORN-KNOP. DATE ABOUT 1400. DUG UP AT COVENTRY.

[V. AND A. M.]

PLATE XXV

1   2   3   4   5

OLD SILVER SPOONS OF ENGLAND

An Exeter Apostle spoon of about 1640, partly gilt, with the figure of St. Matthew, the nimbus moulded with the Saint Esprit, the bowl pricked with the initials F.K. and the date " 1680," went for four-and-a-half guineas. A Commonwealth Puritan bearing the London date-letter for 1656–7, with R. as the maker's mark, sold for seven guineas, with a provincial Puritan, of about 1660, thrown in for good measure.

Numerous other bargains in sixteenth and seventeenth century provincial Seal-tops, seventeenth century Puritans and Lobed-ends, and seventeenth century provincial Apostles—all stamped " Breadalbane " on the backs of the stems—were offered at the same sale.

These relatively trifling incidents of the sale are described because they illustrate forcibly the two points of view, and show incidentally that a collector who really loves old silver spoons need not be rich in order to acquire them, if only he will study his subject in advance, know when to seize bargains when offered, and be content with provincial marks, unascribed marks, or no marks at all.

It may be mentioned that the rare silver-gilt late sixteenth century Seal-top at South Kensington, with the stem and inside of the bowl beautifully engraved with characteristic ornamentation of the period, which is illustrated on Plate XII, was purchased in the ordinary way for fifteen shillings because of its lack of marks. Other collectors scattered all over the country have doubtless acquired similar bargains at a comparatively trivial cost.

It should be borne in mind, however, on the other hand, that the collector who will consider the purchase only of fully-marked London-made spoons has one signal advantage over the snappers-up of unconsidered trifles, provincial or unmarked.

He acquires not only examples of the splendid London craftsmanship,

144

SUGGESTIONS TO COLLECTORS

but, if he is gifted with imagination, he obtains also the definite local "atmosphere" more or less denied to undated specimens.

He knows, for example, that the year which saw the making of his silver-gilt Apostle also saw Shakespeare produce *Hamlet* at the Globe, his Lion Sejant of 1577 Drake on his cruise in the *Golden Hind,* or his Maidenhead of 1588, the year of the Armada, as the case may be.

He realises again, that his Jacobean Seal-top must have been assayed at Goldsmith's Hall within a few months of the sailing of the *Mayflower,* and that his Apostle of 1660, pricked in the bowl with the initials S.P., may have been one of the very six spoons which Pepys is known to have been carrying in his pocket to Walthamstow, together with a silver porringer, on May 29, 1661, to present as a christening gift. The initials pounced on some of these spoons, it is now believed, were often those of sponsors at christenings.

The collector of more modest means, however, who picks up, say, a wistful-looking small Stump-top, with its marks present, but so woefully corroded as to be almost illegible, but with a beautifully engraved head and long face with a vandyke beard, near the top of the front of the stem, and clearly recognisable as that of Charles I, is probably equally correct in his deduction that his trifle was the property of one of Charles' Cavaliers, that the Cavalier buried it for safety when he drew his sword for his King in the Civil War, and that he never returned to retrieve it, the spoon lying underground for centuries until discovered by sheer accident during digging operations.

Scores of London and provincial spoons offer peeps at their chequered histories, apart from their official marks, if only the collector of to-day can decipher and interpret their pounces, scratches, pittings and other scorings.

OLD SILVER SPOONS OF ENGLAND

PLATE XXVI

SHOWING USE OF WOODEN SPOON-STANDS

(1) AND (3) LATE SIXTEENTH CENTURY LION SEJANT.

(2) LATE SEVENTEENTH CENTURY SMALL LOBED-END (DUG UP).

(4) EARLY GEORGIAN FOLDING-SPOON WITH SILVER RAT-TAILED BOWL, AND HORN HANDLE BOUND WITH BRASS.

(IN THE AUTHOR'S COLLECTION.)

PLATE XXVI

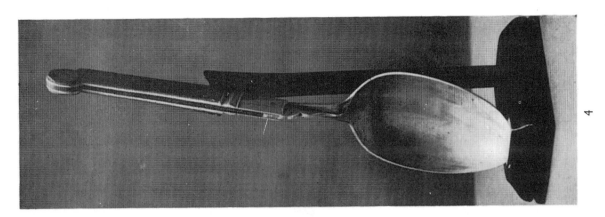

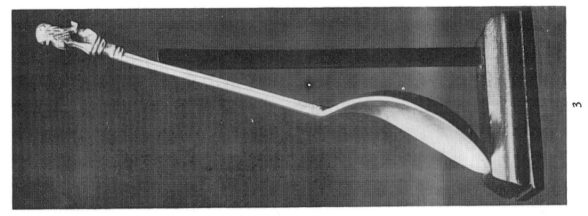

4

3

2

I

SUGGESTIONS TO COLLECTORS

The mutual attitudes of these two broad classes of collectors impress the newcomer to the collecting field very much as the respective attitudes of the Box-and-Stall-holders, on the one hand, and the Galleryites on the other, at a play or grand opera performance.

Both classes of theatre patrons affect a good-humoured disdain for one another.

The Galleryites aver the play's the thing, and that it is sheer folly to waste money on a stall or a box, while the occupiers of the more expensive seats pity the poor Galleryite for his total loss of the social atmosphere of the performance, the sparkling jewels, lovely women, beautiful dresses and well-known persons on view, which, in their eyes, are often a greater attraction than the piece itself.

Similarly with collectors of old silver spoons.

Collectors of small means, but with a delight in ancient silver, declare the spoon's the thing, particularly the knop and the bowl or spoon-self, and that the marks, and even the condition of the spoon, are secondary considerations, provided their own knowledge and instinct convince them the piece is English and authentic.

They assert that it is absurd to pay, perhaps, ten times the price for a spoon because of its good marks and perfect condition.

They suggest, for example, that, for anyone with money to spare, a Tudor cottage in the country is better value than a complete set of Apostle spoons—and both these investments frequently cost about the same.

Well-to-do collectors, on the other hand, avow that a spoon with poor or no marks, Acorn-knops and Diamond-points possibly excepted, is as devoid of distinction, interest, identity and atmosphere alike, as it is bare of proper " touches."

Which class is right ? Probably both.

147

OLD SILVER SPOONS OF ENGLAND

The dealer in ancient silver, in any case, is not to blame. He has to cater to clients of whom a large proportion never fail to remember that they are paying good prices for good marks partly as an investment.

The answer depends on the individual, his means and his sense of the relative values to him of the things in which he delights.

Certain it is that spoons with poor marks do not command the same ready sale as do those with good ones, and that a collector who pays £50 or even £100 for a single spoon at a public auction is more likely to receive his money back when he wishes to sell at the proper time, than the collector who pays only £5 or £10 for a specimen which has no market value because of some fatal flaw in it.

The varieties of spoons to be sought for depend on the taste of the individual collector. Many collect only Apostles, resting content when they have acquired a mixed set of twelve different ones, with a Master, of various dates and makers. As much as £500 is sometimes asked for such a mixed set of early seventeenth century dates.

Some collect only Lobed-ends, others again content themselves with Seal-tops or Slipped-ends, while some find provincials the most fascinating of all. Still others make it their ambition to acquire one good specimen and one only of every known variety of ancient English spoon. A single good example of each of twelve distinct varieties of early English spoons, including one Apostle, would be considered an exceptionally fine collection of this sort, and, failing an expenditure of several hundreds of pounds, might occupy almost a lifetime's quest. Some, further, are interested in any sixteenth century or in any seventeenth century spoon, as the case may be. Many collectors, it may be added, find their taste changes from year to year. These sell or exchange their old loves, just as soon as they find their interest is waning, in favour of the new.

SUGGESTIONS TO COLLECTORS

It is frequently asked, particularly in the absence of any of the orthodox marks :

" How is it possible to tell that an apparently ancient spoon, sold, say at Christie's or a reputable dealer's, is what it purports to be, and, even if it bears apparently ancient marks, that these marks are genuine ? "

There are many answers to reassure the apprehensive would-be collector.

In the first place, the maker of a modern copy of an old silver spoon would have to ensure that the full set of modern hall-marks was punched upon it. The maker and seller of an unmarked modern spoon, whether or not it was a copy of an old one, would be liable to a £10 fine, or in default, imprisonment. One offender in the early years of the present century had to pay fines amounting to more than £3,000 for forging old marks on modern silver, besides forfeiting the offending plate. The making of wrought silver has for centuries been hedged round with drastic penalties. An Act of George II even imposed death as a felon for conterfeiting Hall marks, this extreme penalty materially assisting in putting a stop to frauds.

Secondly, it is practically impossible successfully to imitate the colour, craftsmanship, surface, form and finish of an old English silver spoon and the effects of its centuries of use and existence.

The author recently inspected a pair of copies of ancient Slipped-ends, and a copy of an ancient Puritan, made by an excellent modern craftsman, and the spoons, quite apart from their modern marks, would not have deceived the veriest tyro.

Modern copies of Apostles are sometimes offered for sale at the Caledonian Market, to which the same criticism applies. The copies, of course, must not be punched with a Leopard's Head in the bowl as were the originals.

149

OLD SILVER SPOONS OF ENGLAND

Thirdly, it would not pay a dishonest silversmith to forge, in the bad sense of the verb, even an unmarked old silver spoon.

Fourth, doubtful spoons would not figure in famous collections, and would not be passed as fit for auction or sale by the experts at famous salerooms, or well-known firms with reputations to lose.

Old silver spoons are rarely fraudulently copied. The few modern silversmiths capable of making even passable imitations would be the last to descend to such practices. Doubtful spoons are far more likely to be of Continental origin, a number of old Dutch Apostles and Lobed-ends in particular closely resembling their English equivalents. Copies made from casts taken from genuine old spoons are sometimes encountered, but they neither look nor feel genuine.

Should old English silver spoons be used by their owners at the table?

The concensus of opinion among collectors seems to be that nothing earlier than Georgian eighteenth century spoons should be so employed, except perhaps on some special " State occasion," after which all sixteenth and seventeenth century specimens used should be carefully washed and polished by the owner in person or his wife.

A single careless act by a nervous, negligent or hurried man or maid in clearing away or washing up may bend, break, scratch, tear or do irreparable damage to a cherished specimen.

Many collectors would consider it little less than sacrilege to eat from their treasured pieces, although several titled or landed old English households known to the author still use services of either sixteenth or seventeenth century spoons, which have been in the family for generations, Apostles and those handsome Charles II Lobed-ends with decorated backs being apparently the favourites.

One man and one only in the service of the family is generally personally responsible for the cleaning and care of these precious services.

SUGGESTIONS TO COLLECTORS

The average collector will not care to take this risk of injury.

The spoon-stand offers an excellent way of accommodating early spoons—the word "displaying" is odious, because it implies that the spoons have been acquired for ostentation or making others envious, which no true collector wishes to do.

This stand is shown on Plate XXVI. It is a simple, effective affair of two pieces of wood, painted or lacquered black or dark brown, which may be readily made even by an amateur carpenter.

It consists of a small rectangular base, $1\frac{1}{2}$ by $2\frac{1}{4}$ inches, with a socket cut into the upper part of the rear portion of the base, which is about $\frac{1}{2}$ an inch deep, to take the upright, and a sunken demi-lune about the size of a thumb-nail, in the front portion of the base to prevent the lip of the spoon-bowl slipping.

A thin flat upright piece of wood, less than $\frac{1}{4}$ of an inch wide and $4\frac{1}{4}$ inches showing upright above the base, is inserted in the socket, a depression or "collar" carved in the extreme upper front portion of the upright to support the stem of the spoon, and the stand is complete. Some collectors prefer the ordinary pipe-rack, which, however, has generally the disadvantage of concealing portions of the stems of the spoons.

A few words about the cleaning of old silver spoons. The ordinary strong acid preparations used for cleaning brass, pewter and other base metals should never, in any circumstances, be employed. Neither should the spoons be burnished, the practice with many silversmiths in dealing with modern silver.

The continued use of acid preparations not only injures the precious metal, but gives it a meretricious "face" or surface which may never disappear.

The collector who wishes his old spoons to retain their ancient soft shimmer cannot do better than wash them only in warm soapy water

151

and polish carefully and gently with a piece of soft chamois leather. Some collectors, again, use only the lather from shaving cream, which, because of its fatty content, they declare, gives a soft, rich, unequalled lustre.

Paul de Lamerie's advice, however, although given two hundred years ago, still holds good to-day.

This great craftsman sent out to favoured customers, who had ordered a service of plate from him, not only the famous plate, but such directions for cleaning it as would best preserve its fine lustre and sparkling beauty.

"Clean it now and then," he wrote, "with only warm water and soap, with a spunge, and then wash it with clean water and dry it very well with a soft linnen cloth and keep it in a dry place for the damp will spoyle it . . . by no means use either chalke, sand or salt."

CHAPTER XIII

A Few Notes on Prices

Complexity of the subject—The host of factors that combine to determine the price realised for an early old Silver Spoon—known "pedigree," condition, rarity, competition, &c.—Missing unit in a set of six or twelve and what it means in money—Apostle Spoons made by the prolific unknown maker who used the "Fringed S"—Quest for missing spoons—The set of eight Apostles at the Breadalbane sale—Every specimen of an early Spoon judged on its own merits—No hard-and-fast rule or standard price—Fifteenth Century Spoons at 100 Guineas apiece—How flaws depreciate the value—Diamond-points and Maidenheads—Part which psychology plays in prices of Knopped Spoons—Provincials—Approximate prices of Fifteenth, Sixteenth and Seventeenth Century specimens.

A NUMBER of actual prices have already been quoted in this volume, and I hesitate to approach the subject in more detail lest the figures be misleading.

With eighteenth century silver spoons sold at so much per ounce the problem is relatively simple, but with " early " fifteenth, sixteenth and seventeenth century specimens sold " all at," that is by the piece set, or lot, it becomes highly complex and involved, dependent on a number of qualifying circumstances likely to be overlooked by the collector.

The known " pedigree " of the early spoon, the collecting repute of the individual or family selling it, its condition, size and weight, the

153

NOTES ON PRICES

current state of the antique silver spoon market, which frequently changes almost from week to week, the amateur and professional bidders at the sale, the rarity of the specimen or the punched marks upon it, even the nature of the exceptional pricking or engraving on knop, stem or bowl, the competition of rival bidders, the saleroom where it takes place, these and a host of other similar factors, all combine to determine the price realised. Again, a dealer may have been commissioned by a wealthy British or American collector to secure a choice specimen, whatever the cost. The price realised, because of its unexpected highness —or lowness—often comes with a shock of astonishment to the outsider present at the sale.

Again, an amateur collector or a dealer may have five or eleven of a set of rare spoons all made by the same maker in the same year, and may be anxious to secure just one more specimen of the same year and maker to complete his set, which is thereby rendered far more valuable.

A set of five Charles II, London-made Lobed-ends or Trifids, for example, with the handsome decorated backs, may be already in the possession of one collector. The five may be worth £50, which works out at £10 apiece, but a set of six, on the other hand, might be valued not, as might be expected, at £60, but at £100.

It will be readily understood that such a collector, if he sees by the catalogue that his " missing sixth " has at last found its way into the auction-room, is likely to be a determined bidder at the sale, and possibly run up the price of the spoon.

Apostle spoons illustrate this particular qualification of prices still more forcibly. Consider, for the sake of illustration, the sets of Apostles made about four hundred years ago, more or less, by the mysterious prolific craftsman who used the fringed or spiked S as his only maker's

PLATE XXVII

THREE INTERESTING RAT-TAIL DESSERT-SPOONS

(1) AND (2) SHIELD-TOP OR WAVED-END OF THE TIME OF QUEEN ANNE. MADE BY THOMAS SPACKMAN, LONDON, 1709–10. PRICKED ON BACK OF HANDLE "M.C. 1709, K.C.," POSSIBLY TO COMMEMORATE A MARRIAGE. (FROM THE AUTHOR'S COLLECTION.)

(3) SHIELD-TOP OR WAVED-END OF GEORGE I, WITH A RAT-TAIL ON THE FRONT OF THE HANDLE. LONDON, 1714–15.

(4) A D (5) HANOVERIAN PATTERN GEORGE I RAT-TAIL, SHOWING ROUNDED TURNED-UP END OF HANDLE AND RIB RUNNING DOWN CENTRE OF STEM. LONDON, 1715–16.

[V. AND A. M.]

PLATE XXVII

1   2   3   4   5

mark, and whose " touch " appears from the latter part of the fifteenth century well into the middle of the sixteenth.

These " S " sets, in the course of the centuries, have been dispersed, and are now found in ones, twos or more in private collections scattered all over the country, or else, quite possibly, still lie buried underground.

The acquisition by some fortunate collector of two of one set of thirteen wrought by this maker may fire the collector with a lifelong ambition to increase his set until he possesses the complete and much coveted set of thirteen, all with different Apostle-knops and a Master-knop made by this maker in the same year.

The completion of such a set in the eyes of many an enthusiastic collector would be equivalent to the raising of a Derby winner in the world of horse-racing.

Odd Apostle spoons are frequently found in collections hundreds of miles apart, their owners quite unaware that fellow-owners possess missing spoons of the same or a similar set.

It often remains for the auction-room, following the owner's death or other vicissitude, to bring these sets together after centuries of separation. It should, of course, be pointed out that a Tudor silver-smith or spoon-maker did not confine himself to making one complete set of Apostle spoons in a single year. He may have made several or even many sets in response to the demand for them, and spoons from any one of these sets will to-day be found to " match " with others provided the Apostle has a different knop.

Year by year this quest for the missing spoon proceeds, until another unit is discovered, and those present one day at an auction sale of ancient silver spoons are surprised to note that the price of one particular piece soars unaccountably until it possibly touches a record figure. It is the collector who has found at long last his missing sheep, and is determined it shall escape him no longer.

His object from the commercial point of view will be appreciated when it is mentioned that one Henry VIII Apostle may be sold for less than fifty guineas, whereas a complete set of thirteen may realise the record price of, not 650 guineas, but £4,900, as was the case in July, 1903.

The comparatively low price of 460 guineas fetched for a set of eight Henry VIII Apostles at the Breadalbane sale is thus partly explained, for every one of the eight was stamped at the back of the stem with the name " Breadalbane." This additional stamp, according to prominent collectors attending the sale, not only in itself depreciated the value of the eight, but would more or less stultify any attempt to add to the set until it should reach the complete thirteen. The majority of collectors of Apostle spoons, however, have probably no greater hope or ambition than to acquire a mixed set—twelve different Apostles and a Master, of various dates and makers.

But what, asks the would-be collector, are the average prices realised for particular varieties or sets of fifteenth, sixteenth and early seventeenth century spoons ? Is there no standard figure ?

The reply is—and it cannot be too strongly emphasised—that no hard-and-fast price exists, and that every specimen is judged on its own peculiar merits, and even on its weight if it be unusually heavy.

An attempt may be made, however, in the form of a few notes, to assess the values of ancient spoons in the broadest possible manner, according to the centuries in which they were wrought.

OLD SILVER SPOONS OF ENGLAND

PLATE XXVIII

FIVE EIGHTEENTH CENTURY EXAMPLES

(1) GEORGE I SPOON WITH MARROW-SCOOP HANDLE, THE HANDLE USED FOR EXTRACTING MARROW FROM BONES. LONDON, 1718–19. [V. AND A. M.]

(2) RARE MEDICINE OR CADDY-SPOON WITH STEM IN THE FORM OF A HORSE'S LEG AND HOOF. [L. C.]

(3) GEORGE III FEATHER-EDGE, "OLD ENGLISH" PATTERN TABLE-SPOON. LONDON, 1780–81. [V. AND A. M.]

(4) QUEEN ANNE CADDY SPOON WITH SILVER STEM ATTACHED TO A MOTHER o'PEARL BOWL. LONDON, 1712–13. [L. C.]

(5) GEORGE II HANOVERIAN PATTERN SPOON SHOWING TRANSITIONAL LEAF-DROP AT BACK OF BOWL. LONDON, 1743–4. [V. AND A. M.]

PLATE XXVIII

1   2   3   4   5

NOTES ON PRICES

FIFTEENTH CENTURY

Spoons made in this century furnish links with mediæval times, are extremely rare, and, other things being equal, command exceptionally high prices.

A fifteenth century Master spoon is very rare.

The record price was made by a Master and an Apostle, both of 1490–1, which, as described elsewhere, realised one thousand guineas for the pair in April, 1910.

The following five factors contributed, among others, to this figure :

(a) The spoons were a Fifteenth Century pair, one of the earliest and probably the only such pair known to be in existence.
(b) They were London-made and fully marked.
(c) One of the knops represented the Master.
(d) The spoons were in good condition.
(e) The year in which the auction took place was a good one for selling.
(f) The salesroom was the most famous of its kind in the world and the competition was keen.

Two fifteenth century Apostles, on the other hand, one a St. Andrew of 1492, with a fringed S as the maker's mark, and the other a St. John of 1495, with the same maker's mark, were sold in the same decade for respectively £50 and £90. The complexity of the subject is only too obvious.

Fifteenth century London-made spoons in good condition and properly marked, sold when the market is good and in the proper place, frequently realise 100 guineas for either Wrythens, Acorns, Diamond-points, Maidenheads, Lion Sejants or other rare examples, particularly if the specimen bears the early London assay mark of the uncrowned Leopard's Head.

OLD SILVER SPOONS OF ENGLAND

A Wrythen-knop of 1488–9, as described elsewhere, realised this sum at the Breadalbane sale in May, 1926.

The collector, however, must not rush to the conclusion that his cherished specimen, which he purchased for a few pounds, and which apparently fulfils all the conditions cited, is worth 100 guineas.

The eye of the expert, assisted by the magnifying-glass, will often detect important flaws in the seemingly perfect specimen. The knop may at some time have broken off and have been re-soldered on. The bowl may have curled up or been worn away at the lip by the ancient practice of scraping a plate, pot or basin with it, to help clean the utensil or extract the last possible morsel of food.

This habit, when persisted in for many years, particularly in the case of a thin spoon, has ruined numbers of otherwise beautiful spoon-bowls. The curled-up or worn-away lip may then have been hammered out in an attempt to restore the bowl to its original shape, but the expert is not often deceived.

One of the marks, again, may be very faint, or so worn away with use and cleaning, or by corrosion, due to burial underground or acid cleaning material carelessly left on the spoon, that the mark is illegible.

The absence of a date-letter, where a date-letter should be, particularly depreciates the value of a spoon. The nimbus, or the emblem of an Apostle, may also be damaged or missing, or the bowl may be breaking away from the stem. The collector may discover that his treasure is worth no more than a fraction of the price he hoped for, perhaps ten guineas, or even less.

It is only the extremely good, unusual and well-marked fifteenth century that realises three figures.

A fifteenth century Diamond-point, with its only mark, the

NOTES ON PRICES

uncrowned Leopard's Head in a dotted circle, punched in the bowl, and believed to be London-made, was sold about twenty years ago, as mentioned elsewhere, for £29, and a fine specimen to-day would probably sell for several times that figure.

A Maidenhead, with the same mark, sold about the same time, brought only £15. The reader must draw his own conclusions.

The more fully marked London Maidenhead of 1487–8, also mentioned in another chapter, with a wheel as the maker's mark, which realised £46, would probably fetch more than that sum to-day, but no expert would venture to predict even its approximate price without seeing and handling it.

With provincial fifteenth century spoons the question of probable value is even more involved. Here again, however, it would depend on the spoon's individual merits.

The wonderful Maidenhead from the famous H. D. Ellis collection at South Kensington, and shown on Plate III, stamped on the bowl with the arms of the See of Coventry, would probably fetch considerably more than 100 guineas if put up to auction to-morrow. The mark in the bowl, quite apart from the unusually early character of the whole spoon, knop, stem and bowl alike, gives it an identity lacking in so many provincial unascribed, which bear an unknown maker's symbol or initials and nothing else.

The fifteenth century Woodwose-knop at South Kensington, also shown on Plate III, and described in another chapter, is a further example of a spoon which, so far as is known, is the only one of its kind in existence to-day, and might, if put up to auction, realise a very large sum.

Psychology plays its part in the value of old silver spoons, just as it does in other branches of collecting.

161

NOTES ON PRICES

A would-be owner likes some definite " signature " on a spoon fully as much as he does on an oil painting.

Collectors, unconsciously perhaps, always give preference to a spoon which bears upon its surface, in the form of punches, some token of the personality or identity of its maker, or its town of origin or both.

It is this " personal equation," indeed, which largely accounts for the popularity of spoons knopped with the image of a living creature such as Maidenheads, Lion Sejants and particularly Apostles.

Authentic fifteenth century provincial spoons so rarely come into the market as to make any estimate of their value pure conjecture.

Again, it is impossible, frankly, to estimate even approximately the value of unmarked spoons, although they form a considerable percentage of the spoons ascribed to the fifteenth century and figure largely in many private collections and in the public museums. It may be pointed out that the most valuable ancient English spoon in existence is unmarked. It is, of course, the Anointing Spoon in the Tower.

SIXTEENTH CENTURY

The record for a single spoon, so far as the price is concerned, was reached by the St. Nicholas spoon of 1528–9, described and illustrated elsewhere, which, despite the fact that it only weighed about three ounces, realised £690. The principal factor which contributed to this price was that the spoon was at the time of the sale in 1902, and is to-day, the only old silver spoon known with this peculiar knop, and it was, therefore, considered a unique specimen.

162

OLD SILVER SPOONS OF ENGLAND

PLATE XXIX

FROM THE NATIONAL COLLECTION AT SOUTH KENSINGTON

(1) LARGE AND SMALL GEORGIAN SO-CALLED "OLIVE" SPOONS WITH SLENDER BARBED OR POINTED STEMS, WHICH WERE USED FOR MAKING TEA, THE POINTS TO CLEAR THE SPOUT OF THE TEA-POT AND THE BOWLS FOR STRAINING THE INFUSION.

(2) TEA-SPOONS AND DESSERT-SPOONS WITH THE BACKS OF THE BOWLS EMBOSSED WITH SHELLS, SCROLLS AND FOLIAGE. CHIEFLY LONDON-MADE, MIDDLE AND SECOND HALF OF THE EIGHTEENTH CENTURY.

(3) MARROW-SCOOPS OF GEORGE II AND GEORGE III.

[V. AND A. M.]

PLATE XXIX

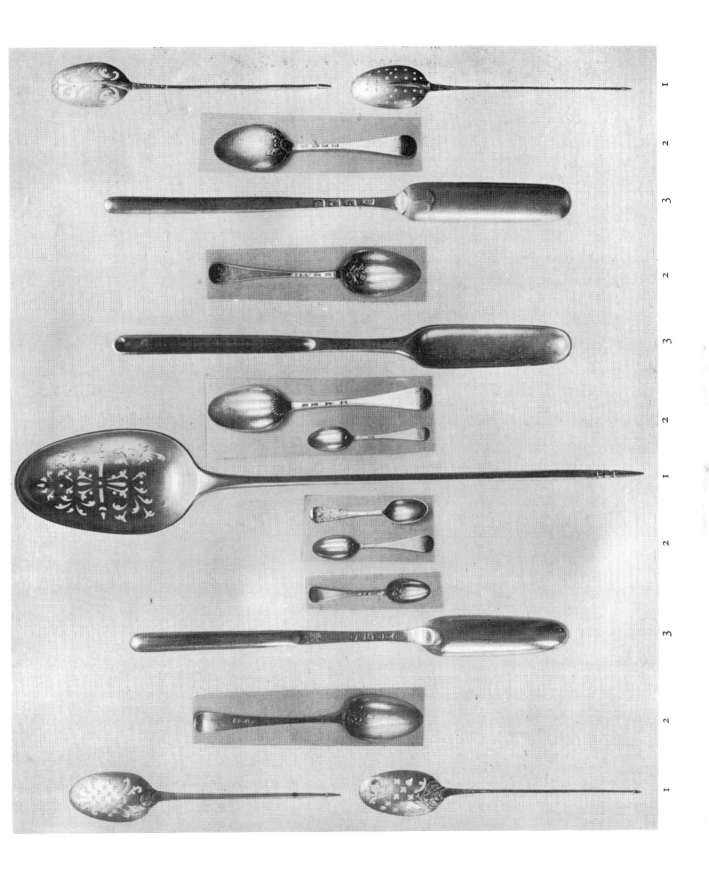

OLD SILVER SPOONS OF ENGLAND

APOSTLES

Henry VIII Apostles realise to-day from fifty to eighty guineas apiece if they fulfil the conditions already mentioned, and Master spoons from 100 guineas upwards. Elizabethan Apostles bring anywhere from twenty-five to forty guineas apiece with fifty to seventy guineas or more for a Master. With Apostles, the character of the Apostle image and the particular maker's mark are important factors, always bearing in mind that this variety of spoon is often acquired to make up sets.

MAIDENHEADS AND LION SEJANTS

The values of these have been sufficiently indicated elsewhere.

SEAL-TOPS

These realise anything from fifteen to forty guineas for good London examples, according to size, date and the form of the seal and baluster. As a general rule the earlier the specimen the higher the value, the earlier octagonal seals bringing more than the round ones, and Baluster-knops, because of their scarcity, more than the ordinary Seal-tops.

Provincials realise from ten guineas upwards.

SLIPPED-IN-THE-STALKS

These often bring anything from twenty-five guineas and upwards, size and gilding being often a factor in the value of this variety, some being unusually large, and others unusually small, while others are entirely covered with the original gilding. An Elizabethan example, inscribed " Capt. Cotton ; made in the Magellan Straits, 1592," etc., realised £56 a few years ago at Christie's.

SEVENTEENTH CENTURY

APOSTLES

These bring twenty-five guineas apiece and upwards for good specimens of the reign of James I, and twenty guineas and upwards for Charles I examples, with Cromwellian about the same figure.

Jacobean Master spoons realise from about forty-five guineas upwards, and Carolean and Cromwellian specimens frequently a little less. Apostles of Charles II, James II, and William and Mary, which are ignored by many collectors, may be obtained from twelve guineas and upwards.

SLIPPED-IN-THE-STALKS

These cost from £20 and upwards for Jacobean, and from fifteen guineas for those of Charles I.

SEAL-TOPS

London examples of James, Charles and Cromwell may be acquired from £10 upwards according to size and condition with provincials frequently at about half that figure. Prices, however, here as elsewhere, vary enormously. A provincial Seal-top of about 1625, made by Timothy Skottowe, of Norwich, realised £44 a few years ago at Christie's.

OLD SILVER SPOONS OF ENGLAND

PURITANS

These realise from £15 upwards for good examples of Charles I, Cromwell and Charles II.

LOBED-ENDS

These bring from £7 upwards for late seventeenth century London examples, the decorated-back spoons of Charles II being valued at £10 and upwards. Beautiful provincial specimens can be obtained from £2 10s.—£3 and upwards.

SHIELD-TOPS AND QUEEN ANNE SPOONS

These can be acquired for from £2 10s. and upwards for excellent London examples.

CHAPTER XIV

LATE OLD SILVER SPOONS FOR DOMESTIC USE

Georgian silver beautiful and inexpensive—£1,000,000 worth of old English silver bought by Americans annually—American old silver at South Kensington—Paul Revere—Queen Mary's gift of teaspoons to the Museum—Extra fine Britannia silver of Anne and early George I—Disappearance of the Rat-tail—The Leaf-Drop—Spoons with decorated backs—The so-called "Olive Spoons" actually used originally to strain infused tea, the point of the stem to clear the spout of the teapot—Spoons now made in all sizes—Tea and snuff-spoons—Caddy spoons—More than 200 varieties of these from which to choose—The "Jockey Cap"—The great Paul de Lamerie, Thomas Harache, Paul Crespin and others all put their "touch" on spoons—Famous women silversmiths and spoonmakers and where they worked—Hints to would-be collectors—Buying by units to make up a set—The best books on the subject of Hall-marks—How to read the Marks—Conclusion.

DISCERNING lovers of old silver spoons acquire, for daily domestic use, specimens of the early eighteenth and nineteenth centuries.

Spoons made in the reigns of Anne, and particularly of George I, George II, George III, and George IV are beautiful and inexpensive—the Georgian cost little more than twentieth century articles and sometimes less. They are also, many of them, substantial, and all still fragrant with history.

Thousands of families in this country, rich and poor alike, take a pride in their old Georgian silver spoons, even if, as in some cases, their " collection " is confined to a single specimen.

PLATE XXX

Tea-Caddy Spoons, Including the Jockey-Cap, Eighteenth and Early Nineteenth Centuries. The Quest of Many Collectors.

[V. AND A. M.]

PLATE XXX

SPOONS FOR DOMESTIC USE

Queen Mary is known to be a connoisseur of Georgian silver, as she is of old furniture, and a beautiful set of twelve very small tea-spoons, bearing the London Hall-mark for 1799–1800, and the maker's mark G.S. (George Smith), presented by her to the nation, may be seen at the Victoria and Albert Museum, with their fascinating red leather case.

It is estimated that £1,000,000 worth of old English silver leaves this country annually for the United States, and the greater part of this million is made up of Georgian silver, including thousands of Georgian spoons, which, because of their antiquity, enter America duty-free.

Other Georgian spoons, however, equally beautiful, emerge from safe deposit vaults, banks, canteens and cupboards in private houses to take their place in the British sale-rooms and dealers' establishments. The supply seems inexhaustible, although, of course, it cannot be so.

It is sometimes stated that Americans love old English spoons, because the United States has no ancient silver of its own. This illusion will be promptly dispelled by a visit to the Lionel Crichton collection of eighteenth century spoons and other American silver (including a plain silver mug with a reeded band, made by the famous Paul Revere, the Rider of the Revolution, who was also a fine silversmith), on exhibition in the Loan Court at South Kensington; but, alas, old American silver is so scarce to-day as to be almost priceless.

Lobed-end, Shield-top and all the other ancient spoons mentioned in the preceding pages, had ceased to be produced when George I ascended the throne, with the exception of an occasional early Georgian Lobed-end which frequently bears provincial marks.

169

OLD SILVER SPOONS OF ENGLAND

The bowl had now become longer and more elliptical, the handle rounded at the end and turned up, the rat's-tail, however, being retained. The fact that this change almost coincided with the accession of the House of Hanover has led to these spoons being described as of the Hanoverian pattern, although, as already mentioned, they were being produced in this country as early as 1705. This pattern continued to be made well into the reign of George III, although the rat-tail, as a general rule, disappeared in the reign of George II, and, on many examples, in the latter part of the reign of George I.

The popularity of the new spoon with the rounded-end, turned-up handle, however, was threatened towards the end of the reign of George II by another variety, which soon swept everything before it and indeed continued to the beginning of the nineteenth century.

This is what is known as the "Old English" variety of spoon, with a more pointed or egg-shaped bowl, the end of the handle turned down instead of up, and the rat's-tail shortened into a drop or shell.

The Feather-edge spoon, illustrated on Plate XXVIII, with the end of the handle turned down, is an example of the "Old English" pattern.

Wonderful craftsmen and craftswomen set their "touch" or maker's mark on these silver spoons.

I am fully aware that many of the ancient famous silversmiths, particularly in Tudor and Stuart times, did not have spoons made on their own premises, but ordered them from the specialists in spoon-making outside. These ancient silversmiths, however, were responsible for the designs of the spoons, they exercised supervision over the spoons' craftsmanship, and punched their own makers' marks on the finished products, selling them as their own make.

Paul de Lamerie, who flourished " att the ' Golden Ball ' " in Great Windmill Street, near the Haymarket, and afterwards in Gerard Street, Soho, in the reigns of Queen Anne, George I, and George II, was hailed as the finest silversmith of his time, and succeeding centuries have gone far to confirm his repute.

De Lamerie, however, was very proud of the spoons he designed, and sold as his own.

An invoice of plate, which he supplied to the Hon. George Treby, Privy Councillor and Secretary of War in the time of Queen Anne, and delivered in the years 1721–25, includes " 4 ladles or ragoos spoons, weigh 27 ozs. 10 dwt. . . . £8 14s. 0d." " 12 knifs, 12 spoons, 12 forks for desert. . . . £15 1s. 5d," and " fashion of ye spoons and forks att 3s. each. . . . £3 12s. 0d."

A " large rat-tail spoon," sold by this master was also marked at Goldsmiths' Hall for 1720–21, and a tablespoon of 1733–4, with his maker's mark, is in the Dasent collection. A number of other examples of his spoons are also on record.

Thomas Harache, again, one of the Royal goldsmiths who flourished in Pall Mall in the reign of George III, and the latter part of the reign of George II, and who was famous for his artistic plate, set his maker's mark of " T.H. Crowned " on spoons.

Spoons and a christening basin bearing his mark, and the date-letter for 1763–4, which formed part of a service for the Prince of Wales, who was afterwards George IV, are in the collection of the Royal Family.

Paul Crespin or Crispine, who is found in the year 1720 flourishing at the " Golden Ball " in Compton Street, Soho, was another famous silversmith of his time whose rat-tailed spoons are sometimes encountered by collectors.

It is fitting that women, to whom old silver makes a special appeal, should have played a considerable part in the London silversmith's craft from early Tudor times right through the centuries, and have left their makers' marks on thousands of spoons that still survive, particularly spoons of the eighteenth century.

Many of the large and growing number of women collectors of old spoons for domestic use now give preference to spoons bearing the maker's marks of silversmiths of their own sex. It is a fascinating hobby, with all sorts of surprises and possible bargains waiting sometimes just round the corner.

An old, old table-spoon, offered for a few shillings, its quaint bowl covered with fine scratches, and one side of the " lip " slightly curled, but with a long, delicate, tapering shaft, may prove to bear the mark of Hester Bateman, a famous London silversmith in the days of George III.

A wistful little teaspoon, again, bought perhaps for as little as half a crown, may show the " touch " of Eliza Tookey or Eliz. Godfrey, other famous craftswomen. A number of women makers' marks have been specially drawn, and are here reproduced for the benefit of these and other collectors.

A pioneer London woman silversmith was Mrs. Agas Hardinge, who is mentioned as early as 1513, the year of Flodden Field, in the reign of Henry VIII. Another was Margery Herkins, of whom the earliest mention was in 1540 in the same reign. Her establishment was in Lombard Street, appropriately enough, where, like many of her fellow craftsmen, she doubtless combined the silversmith's businesss with banking.

SPOONS FOR DOMESTIC USE

The eighteenth, however, was the great century for the woman silversmith, who worked sometimes in business partnership with a man.

Duly registered London women silversmiths, a large number of whom put their makers' marks on spoons, and the year in which they are known to have been practising their craft, include the following, with some of their characteristic marks :—

WILLIAM III

"Goyce Issod, widdow," of Fleet Street	1697
Dorothy Grant, of Southwark	1697
Alice Sheene, of Lombard Street	1700

ANNE

Mary Bainbridge, of Oat Lane	1707

GEORGE I

Sarah Parr, of Cheapside	1720
Ann Tanqueray, of Pall Mall	1720
Phillis Phillip, of Cannon Street	1720
Hester Fawdery, of Goldsmith Street	1727
Mary Johnson, of Noble Street	1727

GEORGE II

Edith Fletcher, of Foster Lane	1729
Eliz. Goodwin, of Noble Street	1729
Jane Lambe, of Shandos Street	1729

SPOONS FOR DOMESTIC USE

Eliz. **EB** Buteux, of Norris Street, St. James's   1731

Mary **M·L** Lofthouse, of Maiden Lane   1731

Mary **MP** Pantin, of Green Street   1733

Sarah Holaday, of Grafton Street   1735
Dinah Gamon, of Staining Lane   1740
Susannah Hatfield, of St. Martin's Lane   1740
Eliz. Jackson   1740
Eliz. Oldfield   1740
Ann Craig (and John Neville), of Norris Street, St. James's   1740
Isabel Pero, of Orange Court   1741
Eliz. Tuite, of Orange Buildings   1741

Eliz. **E·G** Godfrey, Haymarket   1741

Ann Kersill, of Foster Lane   1747
Dorothy Mills, of Saffron Hill   1752
Sarah Buttall, of the Minories   1754

George III
Eliz. Tookey   1771

Hester **HB** Bateman, of Bunhill Row   1774

Eliz. Roker, of Bishopsgate Street   1776
(Peter and) Ann Bateman, of Bunhill Row   1791
(James and) Elizabeth Bland, of Bunhill Row   1791
Alice (and George) Burrows, of Red Lion Street, Clerkenwell   1802

The quaint makers' marks of virtually all these are recorded, and
may often be identified on a beautiful old tea, coffee, dessert, table,
gravy, or caddy spoon.

OLD SILVER SPOONS OF ENGLAND

PLATE XXXI

PLATE XXXI

OLD SILVER SPOONS OF ENGLAND

Men and women collectors who acquire spoons made in the reign of George I before June, 1720, have the advantage not only of possessing inexpensive but prized rat-tailed spoons more than two hundred years old, but spoons made of the extra fine Britannia silver. This is, of course, not to be confused with the base " Britannia metal " which enjoyed its vogue more than a century later.

A Statute of William III, date 1696, was responsible for raising the standard for plate above that of the silver coinage in order to stop the prevailing practice of melting down coins to make silver spoons and other articles. It was ordained that on and after March 25, 1697, no silver-smith should make any article less in fineness than 11 oz. 10 dwts. of fine silver in every pound Troy, the maker's mark not to be his symbol or initials as theretofore, but the first two letters of his surname. It was likewise ordained that the Lion's Head Erased (which appears to be the profile of the head and neck of a lion with the tongue hanging out) and the figure of a woman, commonly called Britannia, be substituted for the Leopard's Head and Lion. The marks of the Britannia Figure and Lion's Head Erased are illustrated in Chapter X (" London Spoon-marks ").

This act remained in force, as already stated, until June 1720, when a new Act of George I had restored the old standard of 11 oz. 2 dwts. fine. Each maker thereafter, who worked in both standards, used the first two letters of his surname for Britannia silver, and his initials for the old or lower standard.

An Act of George II, however, in 1739, because of the confusion caused by the two sets of marks, ordered the destruction of existing marks and the substitution of initials, a practice which continues to this day.

Georgian Rat-tails of Britannia or other silver cost about twenty-five shillings apiece.

SPOONS FOR DOMESTIC USE

The collector who wishes to acquire spoons for a canteen of Georgian silver which looks beautiful, wears the same all through, lasts a lifetime, and is worth not less but more as time goes on, has a wonderful range of choice.

Spoons up to the latter part of the seventeenth century were, with few exceptions, all of the dessert-spoon size, with occasionally a slightly larger specimen.

Not only dessert spoons, however, but table-spoons, gravy-spoons, tea or coffee spoons, soup-ladles, punch-ladles—which cost anywhere from one to twenty guineas apiece—salt and mustard-spoons, basting spoons, marrow-scoops, soup and other spoons, can all be obtained in beautiful examples of Georgian silver, either singly or in sets.

Many of these spoons, particularly those of George II and George III, have part of the backs of the bowls decorated with a shell, foliage, scroll, ship, or other symbol in relief.

There are also dainty tea-straining, mulberry, or olive-spoons, with long slender bodkin-like handles terminating in a point and with perforated or saw-pierced bowls. They cost from about fifteen shillings upwards and bear the marks of silversmiths of the days of the four Georges. These were formerly believed to be punch-straining spoons of the days of the bucks and dandies, the perforated bowls for taking the cloves and other spices from the punch, and the pointed tips of the stems for spearing the floating slices of lemon.

The best proof that they were originally made for use with the tea-pot as already described is found in the fact that ancient tea-caddies handed down from one generation to another each contain one of these " olive " spoons, with a pair of nippers or sugar-tongs and a caddy-spoon.

OLD SILVER SPOONS OF ENGLAND

PLATE XXXII

SILVER PUNCH-LADLES OF EIGHTEENTH AND EARLY NINETEENTH CENTURIES.
FROM THE J. H. FITZHENRY GIFT. (LENGTHS FROM 9 TO 16 INCHES).

(1) WITH WHALEBONE HANDLE. LONDON, 1746–7. MAKER'S MARK W.

(2) WITH EBONY HANDLE. ENGRAVED WITH THE CREST OF BRANDLING OF NORTHUMBERLAND. MADE BY SAM MERITON "AT YE ANCHOR" IN HUGGIN ALLEY, WOOD STREET, LONDON, 1753–4.

(3) CHASED AND *Repoussé* WITH WHALEBONE HANDLE. BOWL BEATEN OUT OF COIN AND SET WITH GILT SHILLING OF 1711.

(4) CHASED AND *Repoussé* WITH WHALEBONE HANDLE. BOWL BEATEN OUT OF CROWN PIECE, AND SET WITH SHILLING OF 1723.

(5) CHASED AND *Repoussé* WITH WHALEBONE HANDLE. BOWL BEATEN OUT OF COIN.

(6) CHASED AND *Repoussé*, THE INSIDE GILT. MARKS, LEOPARD'S HEAD (REPEATED), LION PASSANT AND I.W. WITH QUATREFOIL AND PELLET. LONDON, MIDDLE OF EIGHTEENTH CENTURY.

(7) CHASED AND *Repoussé*, WITH WHALEBONE HANDLE. BOWL BEATEN OUT OF COIN.

(8) BOWL BEATEN OUT OF CROWN-PIECE AND SET WITH SHILLING OF 1711.

(9) WITH FLUTED BOWL AND WHALEBONE HANDLE (FRENCH).

(10) BOWL SET WITH GEORGIAN SIXPENNY PIECE.

(11) BOWL BEATEN OUT OF CROWN-PIECE. LATE EIGHTEENTH CENTURY.

(12) SCOTCH. GLASGOW, 1863–4. MAKER'S MARK J.M. (J. MURRAY).

PLATE XXXII

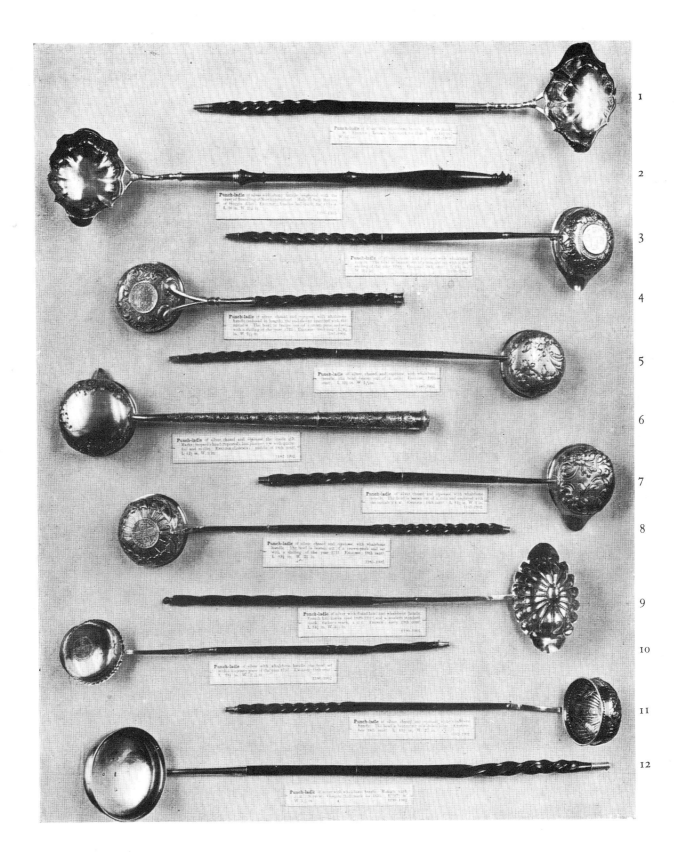

1

2

3

4

5

6

7

8

9

10

11

12

SPOONS FOR DOMESTIC USE

Many of the smaller varieties of Georgian spoons because of their slight weight were permitted to bear three and even two marks only—the maker's mark and the lion.

Much sought after are the early diminutive snuff-spoons, which came in with the introduction of snuff-taking in the time of Queen Anne, when Sir George Rooke captured enormous quantities of snuff in Vigo Bay, the spoons being used both by men and women of fashion to extract the snuff from the *étui* in which it was generally carried. They sometimes cost £2 or more apiece because of their rarity.

Some of the varieties of beautiful eighteenth and early nineteenth century spoons of all sorts that may be acquired by collectors of modest means are shown on various Plates in this volume. The illustrations convey a better idea than any worded description.

They include caddy-spoons, of which there are more than two hundred varieties at South Kensington. These spoons are always of small size to fit the tea-caddy in which they were kept under lock and key. They cost anywhere from 7s. 6d. to £5, the price frequently asked for the rare Jockey Cap shown with numerous others on Plate XXX. The collection of Caddy-spoons is the unending quest of many collectors of eighteenth and nineteenth century silver.

Old soup-ladles and gravy-spoons may be obtained from the time of Queen Anne, sugar-sifters, sauce-ladles and marrow-scoops from the days of George I. Most collectors of discrimination sedulously avoid the spoons of all sorts with fiddle-pattern handles which came in during the latter part of the reign of George III, and persist to this day. They also shun the florid nineteenth century so-called " Kings Pattern " variety of this spoon.

Both men and women who wish to acquire sets of late old silver spoons for domestic use can either visit the establishments of well-known

179

OLD SILVER SPOONS OF ENGLAND

LONDON DATE LETTERS FROM 1697 TO 1875 MARKED ON OLD SILVER SPOONS

1697	1701	1706	1711	1716	1721	1726	1731	1736	1741	1746	1751
				A	F	L	Q	a	f	l	q
				B	G	M	R	b	g	m	r
				C	H	N	S	c	h	n	s
				D	I	O	T	d	i	o	t
				E	K	P	V	e	k	p	u
1700	1705	1710	1715	1720	1725	1730	1735	1740	1745	1750	1755

1756	1761	1766	1771	1776	1781	1786	1791	1796	1801	1806	1811
A	F	L	Q	a	f	l	q	A	F	L	Q
B	G	M	R	b	g	m	r	B	G	M	R
C	H	N	S	c	h	n	s	C	H	N	S
D	I	O	T	d	i	o	t	D	I	O	T
E	K	P	U	e	k	p	u	E	K	P	U
1760	1765	1770	1775	1780	1785	1790	1795	1800	1805	1810	1815

1816	1821	1826	1831	1836	1841	1846	1851	1856	1861	1866	1871
a	f	l	q	A	F	L	Q	a	e	l	q
b	g	m	r	B	G	M	R	b	g	m	r
c	h	n	s	C	H	N	S	c	h	u	s
d	i	o	t	D	I	O	T	d	i	o	t
e	k	p	u	E	K	P	U	e	k	p	u
1820	1825	1830	1835	1840	1845	1850	1855	1860	1865	1870	1875

NOTE—The Court-Hand "a", the first letter in the above table, was used from March 27 to May 29, 1697 and the Court-Hand "b", the second letter, from May 29, in the same year, to May 28, 1698. The above date-letters, with this exception, were changed annually on May 29. The date denoted by 1701, in the above table, for example, means from May 29, 1701 to May 28, 1702.

SPOONS FOR DOMESTIC USE

firms who deal in ancient silver, and make their choice of individual spoons or sets—and the prices asked even by famous Bond Street firms are frequently more modest than those of obscure " antique " shops— or else, like the collectors of early spoons, they can master their subject and set out to discover bargains for themselves. They will, in either case, appreciate their beautiful hand-wrought silver far more if they master its relatively simple marks and learn to read its date and maker for themselves.

A book, such as Chaffer's little 7s. 6d. manual of British Hall Marks which contains all the essential tables of marks, apart from the makers' marks, will well repay a study. So, too, will the wonderful collection in the Victoria and Albert Museum at South Kensington.

Those who wish to know something of the personalities of the ancient silversmiths should obtain Chaffers and Markham's *Hall Marks on Gold and Silver Plate*.

The page of annual London date-letters, from the end of the seventeenth century until 1875, presented herewith, will alone enable the collector of late old silver spoons to fix the dates in which his or her acquisitions were made, and will materially enhance their interest. For those wishing to identify the maker a book such as Mr. W. J. Cripps' *Old English Plate* is recommended.

Some of the alphabets of different cycles will appear, at first glance, to the beginner to be the same, but a closer study will reveal marked differences.

The alphabets of 1716 to 1735, and 1796 to 1815, for example, seem almost identical, but a more careful examination will show that the upper corners of the shields of the later alphabet are clipped off, and that the lower extremity of the shield, instead of presenting a regular

181

SPOONS FOR DOMESTIC USE

angle, as in the earlier alphabet, is made up of two curves meeting in the centre and making a bracket.

Similar marked distinctions will be noticed in the other alphabets, which will well repay detailed study.

The marks on the backs of old silver spoons are by no means difficult to understand. The accompanying sketch shows the five characteristic marks grouped together in the back of the handle of a beautiful Georgian " old English " pattern dessert-spoon purchased for less than ten shillings.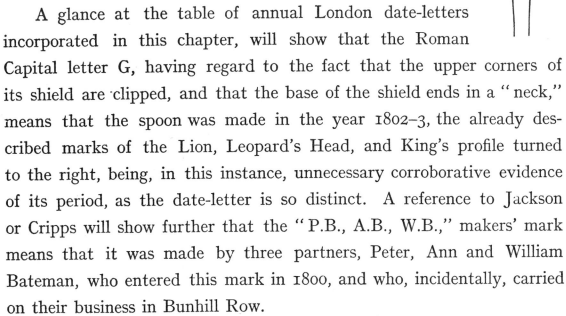

A glance at the table of annual London date-letters incorporated in this chapter, will show that the Roman Capital letter G, having regard to the fact that the upper corners of its shield are clipped, and that the base of the shield ends in a " neck," means that the spoon was made in the year 1802–3, the already described marks of the Lion, Leopard's Head, and King's profile turned to the right, being, in this instance, unnecessary corroborative evidence of its period, as the date-letter is so distinct. A reference to Jackson or Cripps will show further that the " P.B., A.B., W.B.," makers' mark means that it was made by three partners, Peter, Ann and William Bateman, who entered this mark in 1800, and who, incidentally, carried on their business in Bunhill Row.

But, suppose, it may be asked, the date-letter had been worn away, or the spoon had never been punched with a date-letter, the frequent practise with very small light-weight spoons ?

The form of the spoon, with its " old English " pattern, the fact that the makers entered this mark in 1800, would alone combine to fix the approximate date of the spoon, apart from any other marks.

OLD SILVER SPOONS OF ENGLAND

The practice of buying Queen Anne and Georgian spoons by the set is, if easier, a far more expensive method than the gradual acquisition of ones and twos of the same design, but different makers, until a full " set " of six or twelve is obtained.

The sum of £75 may frequently be asked for a fine set of six Queen Anne rat-tailed dessert spoons, all by the same maker and of the same date, and from £50 to £100 for a set of twelve, against £15 for six, and £30 for twelve well-matched similar spoons of various makers and dates.

A set of a dozen Rat-tails of George I, again, may bring from £40 to £70, against £12 or £15 for an " odd," but well-matched dozen. These figures are based on actual recent auction-sales in London.

A dozen larger Queen Anne or George I Rat-tailed table-spoons may realise from £40 to £50, but a dozen " odd " Rat-tail table-spoons of George I, on the other hand, may be frequently acquired for about one-third of that figure—all well-matched and of the same design, but bearing various date-letters and makers' marks.

Single spoons are, other things being equal, the most inexpensive of all. They sometimes cost only a few shillings apiece, and offer a fascinating quest to both men and women collectors of modest means who wish to build up sets for household use.

Such collectors are advised to study the subject of marks for themselves, and to visit the South Kensington Museum, if only to decide which pattern or design most chimes with their individual taste.

Examples by Hester Bateman, Eliza Tookey, and other famous Georgian silversmiths of both sexes, are far from uncommon.

A few suggestions to such collectors may be summarised as follows :

1. Do not buy spoons which show no marks or series of marks which cannot be identified in the standard books on old English silver-marks. Such spoons

OLD SILVER SPOONS OF ENGLAND

are not nearly so interesting, or nearly so valuable to sell again, if the need or occasion arises. They may not be English or silver at all—merely silver-plate.

This warning does not apply, of course, to Scotch or Irish spoons with proper marks, which are well worthy of collection, particularly Irish specimens that are eagerly sought and treasured by discerning collectors.

2. Do not be deceived into buying Continental silver as English, Scotch or Irish. Continental silver is incidentally not nearly as valuable and the marks are not infrequently forged.

3. If you acquire individual spoons with the ultimate object of making a set of six or twelve see that they match. Buy, for example, only Rat-tails, only spoons that are quite plain in design, or only spoons whose handles have a feather border, such as that shown on Plate XXVIII.

4. Do not attempt to make sets of miscellaneous pieces that harmonise neither in size, pattern nor design.

5. Do not, if you can avoid it, buy the late old spoons with "fiddle-pattern" handles which are generally avoided by discriminating collectors.

6. Do not use ordinary polishes for your old silver. Many of these contain strong acids. A good silver preparation has jeweller's rouge as its basis. Warm water and soap are probably the best cleansers of all. Dry with a fine linen cloth and polish with a chamois leather. De Lamerie's recipe, printed in a preceding chapter, still holds good to-day.

What tales of towers, what banquet tunes
What fairy bells and fragrant runes
Of lives and loves in far-off Junes—
Old Silver Spoons!

THE END

INDEX

INDEX

INDEX

INDEX

INDEX

INDEX